Praise for *The Four Gifts of Anxiety*

"This book brings perspective and understanding to what makes us human. The journey of this book moves one from feeling broken to being whole."
—Cindy Horgan, Cohost of the Television Show *Thriving from Anxiety*

"This book is a gift to those living with anxiety. Through practical strategies and powerful insights, you'll learn how to embrace the wisdom that lies underneath the symptoms and focus on the true messages of healing your body is trying to convey."
—Jill Hope, Founder and Empowerment Coach at ishinekids.com

The

FOUR
GIFTS

of

ANXIETY

Embrace the Power
of Your Anxiety and
Transform Your Life

SHERIANNA BOYLE, MED, CAGS

Adams Media
New York   London   Toronto   Sydney   New Delhi

Adams Media
An Imprint of Simon & Schuster, Inc.
57 Littlefield Street
Avon, Massachusetts 02322

For information about special discounts for bulk purchases, please contact Simon & Schuster Special Sales at 1-866-506-1949 or business@simonandschuster.com.

The Simon & Schuster Speakers Bureau can bring authors to your live event. For more information or to book an event contact the Simon & Schuster Speakers Bureau at 1-866-248-3049 or visit our website at www.simonspeakers.com.

Manufactured in the United States of America

10 9 8 7 6

Library of Congress Cataloging-in-Publication Data has been applied for.

ISBN 978-1-4405-8294-3
ISBN 978-1-4405-8295-0 (ebook)

CONTENTS

ACKNOWLEDGMENTS

I dedicate this book to the millions of men, women, young adults, and children who suffer from or who have been negatively impacted by the symptoms of anxiety. Also, to my husband, Kiernan, and our three creators, Megan, Mikayla, and Makenzie. Also, to my mother, Judy; Larry, my father; and my brother, Joe.

INTRODUCTION

If you or someone you know experience anxiety, you might have seen the title of this book and said to yourself, Anxiety, a gift?! I don't think so. Anxiety can cause you to feel misunderstood, underappreciated, and overextended. As a result, you might give up your dreams, develop an "I can't" or "not now" attitude, dissolve businesses, burn out in your job, face financial hardship, live in pain, and end relationships. Anxiety is tied to emotions of guilt and shame, high expectations, daily demands, and pressure. A gift?

Yes, it is true. Anxiety and its symptoms are not inherently "the problem"—the problem is seeing and interpreting those symptoms in a negative way. If you see them as a problem, then that is what they will be. If you see them as guidance, as a road map to gifts already present within you, then *that* is what they will be. The symptoms of anxiety—such as all-consuming thoughts, negativity, and withdrawal—can actually help you unearth positive attributes inside you, waiting to be discovered. This book shows you how to see your anxiety symptoms not as a burden but as an opportunity to discover four extraordinary gifts. Instead of feeling ashamed, weak, stressed out, or held back, you'll now feel **purposeful, resilient, hopeful**, and **empathetic**. These four gifts will change your life.

Imagining yourself with those gifts is difficult if you're alone in the throes of anxiety. After all, anxiety is a lonely journey. Yet if you experience the effects of anxiety in your daily life, you're far from alone. According to the Anxiety and Depression Association of America, anxiety disorders are the most common psychiatric illnesses impacting adults and children. An estimated 40 million American adults suffer from an anxiety disorder and only about one-third receive treatment. Where you fall within those statistics does not matter—what matters is that you're now open to seeing your life in a new light.

The gifts I'll explain in *The Four Gifts of Anxiety* are free, abundant, and accessible to everyone. To access them, however, you must know how to look beyond the surface of your emotions and your life. I'll coach you through the process, showing you different ways to truly get in touch with your sensations, thoughts, beliefs, memories, and emotions. The magnificent gifts of your mind, body, and spirit—purpose, resilience, hope, and empathy—are both your incentive and reward.

The first step on our journey is to learn more about anxiety. When is anxiety "normal" and even helpful? What messages are the common symptoms of anxiety trying to convey to you? Next, you'll learn techniques for using your own energy to transform the symptoms of anxiety. When you know how to quiet your mind and listen to your body, you'll be able to receive the gifts awaiting you. Finally, I'll delve into each of the four gifts—purpose, resilience, hope, and empathy—in more detail.

Sprinkled within each chapter are Gift Tags. Each tag offers a skill, exercise, meditation, or reflection that will help you strengthen your ability to see your life in a new light. Practice them daily, and you will begin to perceive the symptoms of anxiety as potential opportunities to open up to the experience of converting symptoms into gifts.

Within each chapter, you'll also hear stories of other individuals who have transformed their view. Like you, they thought their anxiety was a part of who they were, beyond their control—a weakness they would rather not deal with. Like you, they also knew their life needed to change to some degree to create the life they truly wanted. Their stories will let you know that you're not alone—they made it through, and so will you.

A life with your gifts does not mean a life without challenges, vulnerability, or pain. Instead, a life with your gifts allows you to become empowered by the very same symptoms you once believed disempowered you. Unearthing your gifts comes with great insight into how memories and unpleasant feelings have played a role in how you handle life today. *You will always have a choice to focus either on your symptoms or the gifts that reside within them.* Your symptoms, when honored and experienced, are always worth something.

Your symptoms are actually your ticket to freedom. However, like a show, if you do not bother to attend, you are likely to miss what the event had to offer. By noticing and allowing yourself to experience these symptoms, you are opening yourself up to the gifts within them.

These gifts exist in each and every one of us. Yours (and mine) were delivered through the symptoms of anxiety. I assure you, by the end of this book, *how* your gifts surfaced will not matter to you. What will matter is your ability and willingness to receive them.

PART 1

ANXIETY: WHAT IT IS AND WHAT IT ISN'T

Anxiety is an emotion of unease, uncertainty, and worry about the future. For many it is a way to cope with the demands of life. Anxiety is not your truth, nor is it a way to control or prevent what is happening. It is a limited part of your experience, a fraction of what you are capable of. There is so much more to understand, know, and learn.

CHAPTER 1

WHAT IS ANXIETY?

"And the day came when the risk to remain tight in a bud was more painful than the risk it took to blossom."

—COMMONLY ATTRIBUTED TO ANAÏS NIN, AUTHOR

Anxiety, Defined

True anxiety is a natural human emotion that alerts you to danger or a perceived threat. Without anxiety, you would not be able to handle true emergencies. Anxiety sends your body in a "fight or flight" mode, ensuring your survival on a very basic level. This is not the kind of anxiety most people deal with every day, however.

Psychological Anxiety

The Four Gifts of Anxiety covers symptoms of anxiety that run on autopilot in your body. These symptoms are psychological and physiological in nature. Most of us have experienced this type of anxiety in some form or another many times in our lives. Anxiety is when you can't find your keys and you are rushing around frantically trying to find them thinking you are going to be late and snapping at anyone and anything that gets in the way. You then drive white-knuckled down the road, determining the quality of your day by the number of green lights you pass through. You think about all the things you have to do, what you'd prefer not to do, and the things you really want to be doing.

For many, it isn't until the symptoms of anxiety come on strong that it is even truly noticed. A string of restless nights, disgruntled relationships, weight gain, illness, depression, and poor work performance are some of the ways anxiety can make itself known.

Whether short-term (when you worried while waiting for the result of a medical test) or longer-term (fear over whether or not you are a "good" parent or have saved enough money for retirement), anxiety can present itself in many ways. When feeling anxious, you might experience psychological effects such as:

- Fear
- Worry
- Uneasiness

- Nervousness
- Distress
- Dread
- Self-doubt
- Irritability
- Difficulty sleeping
- Frustration or anger
- Edginess

These emotions can lead to physiological responses such as:

- Increased heart rate
- Perspiration
- Fatigue
- Muscle tension
- Stomachaches
- Poor memory recall

These symptoms of anxiety come and go for most of us. After an event passes, so do the feelings of anxiety that surrounded it. If you're an "anxious person," however, you probably find that you frequently experience situations that cause these symptoms. Your anxiety might affect you almost every day, with varying degrees of severity. Most people with anxiety are able to continue their day-to-day activities despite the fear, tension, and irritability it creates for them.

When Anxiety Gets Out of Hand

If you find yourself unable to function on a daily basis because of your anxiety, it may have progressed to a more severe level.

Consider getting help from a qualified professional—it can only help. Stand up for your right to live a happy, healthy existence. Never let the stigma or shame of getting support stand in your way. All of the strategies in this book are forms of self-support that will help you as well.

An official diagnosis of an anxiety disorder is likely to be based on four main factors:

1. **Frequency:** How often do the symptoms occur?
2. **Duration:** How long do the symptoms last?
3. **Intensity:** How strong are your symptoms?
4. **Impact:** How much do the symptoms impact your everyday life?

Questions that may help you determine the intensity, frequency, and duration are:

- Are you able to work or go to school?
- Can you maintain healthy relationships?
- Do you have any trouble sleeping or concentrating?
- Are you able to find pleasure in your life?

Whether anxiety is new for you or you've experienced it nearly all your life, it's never too late to start addressing your symptoms. Just like when you have a cold, it is always better to give yourself a little tender loving care right away instead of waiting until the cold develops into something worse. Overlooking or ignoring your symptoms commands your brain and body to behave as if all situations are urgent and potentially dangerous. Your neurotransmitters repeat the same pathways (cell-to-cell communication) despite the fact that there is no imminent danger. Therefore, part of the process of accessing your gifts is for you to learn how to clear and retrain your brain and body so that your natural, more relaxed state takes precedence over anxiety. The following table shows you the reactions you're having now and what you can look forward to learning from your anxiety.

Survival Focused	Gift Focused
Fight, flight, freeze response	Living in the present, self-observation
Stress hormones activate	Stress-hormone levels decrease
Heart rate is erratic	Heart rate is smooth and consistent
Feel-good neurotransmitters (e.g., serotonin, GABA) decrease	Feel-good neurotransmitters increase
Short, shallow breaths	Deeper, fuller breaths
Difficulty digesting food, weight loss or gain	Able to read bodily cues for signs of hunger and fullness more clearly
Quick, rushed decisions and actions	Conscious, mindful movements and actions
Moody, or think of worst-case scenario first	Trusting, believing, and seeing good
Pressure, bodily tension	Expansion, release, surrender, flow
Nervous about the future	Grateful for the moment
Surviving on fear	Expanding with love

The synchronicity of your internal systems (respiratory, physical, emotional, muscular skeletal, spiritual, hormonal, energetic, etc.) provide a life of balance. If one system is feeling overpowered while another is doing very little, eventually your body will begin to complain. It complains through your moods, sleep cycles, and behaviors. As a result, you feel like you have one hand on a wheel while the other hovers over a panic button. Your body's physical responses—which were originally meant to be used in extreme situations to ensure basic survival—are now triggered every time you experience anxiety. The good news is, no matter what level of anxiety you experience, you can still access your gifts.

Your Body on Autopilot

My client Amelia's experiences illustrate how common it is for people who struggle with anxiety to feel overpowered by their body's physical reactions. Amelia had been in a relationship with a man for eighteen years. One day, he announced he was ending the relationship and left the home they were living in. Amelia was beside herself. She fluctuated between anger and crying. However, the most intrusive symptom was her thoughts. She paced the floors of her home, wringing her hands, panicking about the future. What would she do if he didn't return? How could she possibly live without him? These thoughts went on for days, affecting her ability to sleep, eat, and remember. One day, she returned home after an errand and realized she never closed the garage or front door of her home. Her body felt achy and her chest, neck, and shoulders were in knots.

Amelia's anxiety is clearly rooted in her relationship crisis. Yet her body reacted as if her life were being threatened. Her symptoms of increased heart rate, nervousness, panic, and preoccupation with the future led her to believe her life was falling apart. Although her life was in no imminent danger, her body responded as if a tiger were approaching her in the wild. Her heart had been broken and she was experiencing a tremendous shock—but she was not in life-threatening danger.

The Dangers of Long-Term Anxiety

In the short term, "running on" anxious symptoms can be an addictive way to push yourself through the day. You may appear on the outside like you are a superhero, taking on tasks and getting the job done. However, as anxiety persists over time, your body eventually speaks up, through sore muscles, pain, discomfort, fatigue, poor sleep, feeling overworked, unhealthy habits, breakdown in relationships, and a disconnection from self. As mentioned earlier, when these symptoms are frequent, chronic (lasting for months), and intense, and they interfere with your ability to function in daily life, mental health professionals and physicians will likely consider a diagnosis of anxiety disorder.

If you don't address your symptoms of anxiety, the buildup can lead to behaviors that on the outside are counterproductive, but on the inside serve as a source of protection. For example, if you were anxious about finishing a final paper for a class, you might hand in the paper early and incomplete as a way to halt the inner experience of anxiety. On the outside, it may appear that you are not trying or didn't study. However, you are choosing to stop the cycle of thought, dread, and worry even if it means you have to suffer the consequences of a poor grade. This type of buildup can also cause you to give in to demands or allow your beliefs to be negotiated. Inside, you may really not agree with your teenager's habits; however, the thought of addressing them (and increasing your anxiety in the process) makes letting the behaviors go unattended more appealing. Learning how to appreciate the gifts anxiety is offering you will help you avoid these unfortunate compromises in your success and your values.

Is Anxiety Truly Bad for You?

Anyone who grew up in the eighties was exposed to the "fat free" fad. All fats were considered bad and dangerous to your health. Later, research showed that the elimination of "healthy" fats such as omega-3 was silently depriving brains and bodies of vital nutrients. Living a completely fat-free lifestyle turned out to be inadvisable. Likewise, should an anxiety-free lifestyle really be your goal?

Instead of trying to cut anxiety out of your life, imagine if you could learn to appreciate the symptoms of anxiety. Consider this: *Anxiety can teach you how to improve your life.* Its symptoms have more potential and ability than previously given credit for. Contrary to what many believe, anxiety can be a gift of growth and change. You just don't yet know how to interpret the red flags that anxiety is waving at you. That's what this book will teach you.

Each emotion you experience is a road sign along your life's path. Even the ones that have been given a bad rap, such as guilt and shame, can point you in the right direction. Instead of ignoring or suppressing each emotion through behaviors such as thinking, you can process the messages they carry. (We'll talk more about these messages in the next chapter.)

Above all, anxiety and its symptoms are reminders that you have free will. You can choose to respond in ways that help your body feel safe. As you learn to center yourself rather than distract yourself, you will find that addressing and clearing away underlying issues does not need to be distressing. Instead, you become empowered by your ability to be your body's teacher, friend, and greatest ally. Positioning yourself in this way allows you to make productive and peaceful choices.

Many people have been taught—consciously or subconsciously—to suppress, ignore, or push away unpleasant feelings. However, as you will learn in this book, those feelings contribute to the process of connecting you to your soul. Connecting to your emotions and analyzing them are vastly different. Dr. Joe Dispenza speaks to this in his book *Breaking the Habit of Being Yourself*. He discusses how connecting to your feelings brings you into a state of balance, while analyzing feelings may drive you out of balance. Choosing to become aware and feel what your body is trying to tell you—without judgment—is what enables you to experience the gifts your anxiety is waiting to give you.

Gift Tag

Reflection: Passion

Have you ever considered that the symptoms of anxiety are your body's attempt to reconnect you to your passions? Take a moment and reflect on what you are passionate about. If you have trouble coming up with the answer, take a moment and reflect on your childhood. What did you love to do? What places, moments, and experiences made you feel the most connected and alive? Do any of those still exist in some form in your life today? If not, imagine what your life would be like if they did.

Where Does the Negativity Come From?

If anxiety can actually be a productive thing, why does it get such a bad reputation in our culture? The truth is that despite all of its press, scientific studies, and medical concerns, psychological anxiety continues to be a silent, often ignored state of functioning. If and when it is brought to the attention of a medical professional, friend, teacher, or therapist, most likely it is presented as "this is what is wrong with me." Rarely does anyone choose to see anxiety as portraying what is right.

Much of the negativity surrounding anxiety traces back to the original interpretations of anxiety. Records dating back as far as the fourteenth century report its symptoms as a sign of:

- Weakness
- Failure
- Inadequacy
- Unworthiness
- Neurotic behavior (according to psychoanalyst Sigmund Freud)

Those descriptors do not exactly make you feel cool, confident, and balanced. Thus, anxiety isn't something you are inclined to advertise on your resume, business card, or Facebook page. If you mention anxiety casually—perhaps to colleagues, other parents, or coworkers—they may acknowledge its presence with a knowing nod, sympathetic look, or meaningless comment. These types of responses silence the emotions that feed the symptoms. Left unattended, emotions like anger, guilt, unworthiness, and shame are stored, rather than approached, never really giving you the chance to see the gifts behind them.

Is Your Response to Anxiety Inherently Negative?

Negativity can also surface in the ways you choose to respond to the worrisome chatter or fear that anxiety brings. If you ignore or disregard the root of the symptoms, you're probably increasing the negative associations you have with anxiety. Let's say you're worried about finishing a complicated work project on time. If you decide to vent about it to your colleagues (instead of buckling down to get it done), you're adding layers of negativity to the situation. Plus, you're inadvertently spreading your anxiety around the office. Taking an objective look at your reactions to anxiety can help you see how you have an opportunity to make them much healthier.

The symptoms of anxiety are not the problem. How you choose to see them determines whether or not negativity and stress arise. The energy present in your body speaks volumes about your response. Your emotions are actually made up of energy—a vibration of molecules and atoms. When this energy is in motion your feelings, thoughts, and actions tend to be more positive and you feel capable and strong. When your energy is stagnant or heavy, you may feel tired, irritable, or negative. Psychological symptoms such as dread and self-doubt are denser emotions. That is why they can sometimes feel like a physical burden to carry.

Emotions are heaviest when you store them in your body. Similar to a drawer stuffed with clothing, over time you forget what is even inside it and some pieces may have gotten lost behind or underneath the drawer; the drawer might get jammed, lopsided, or broken. Your symptoms of anxiety are the same if you keep them stuffed inside your body. In Chapters 4–6 you'll learn how to energetically clean out your body. Changing how you approach your feelings shows you that it's your response to your emotions—not the emotions themselves—that lead to negativity.

Other Common Negative Associations

Your negative associations with anxiety might also come from your experiences with anxious family members or friends. Living with people experiencing anxiety is rarely interpreted as a blessing. Known for its contagious qualities, symptoms such as worrying can often spark negative behaviors such as yelling, blaming, and avoidance. If you've been in the presence of that type of behavior, you likely look at your own anxiety as something to hide or be ashamed of.

Anxiety can also be associated with negative emotions because it reminds you of something painful. People, things, sounds, and sights can serve as painful reminders of unfinished tasks, unpleasant thoughts, uncomfortable feelings, difficult conversations, or past hurt and pain. The very same place you call home, work, or school becomes a trigger for emotional distress. The negative undertone associated with these symptoms blocks the courage, curiosity, and willingness to truly process your anxiety. Instead, you may resort to reacting to and "treating" the symptoms rather than allowing yourself to experience them.

The Connection Between Stress and Anxiety

The Anxiety and Depression Association of America explains that "stress is a response to a threat in a situation," while "anxiety is a reaction to the stress." Stress impacts each and every organism on the planet. It is one of the commonalities between humans, animals, mother earth, and the universe at large. Stress can also be defined as a demand placed on an organism in its ability to adapt and cope with a situation. In other words, stress is part of the living experience. Think about it: You are constantly being asked to cope and adapt in some way. Nothing ever remains the same, and if you attempt to control change, you will only introduce more stress into your life.

Another connection between anxiety and stress is that they are often driven by fears and worries that are not likely to actually happen. In fact, the vast majority of stressors you are anxious about will never come true. You may never get hit by a car, lose your job, or develop that rare disease you read about online. Yet your body and mind still react as if they're imminent dangers.

Your reaction is highly dependent on how you interpret or come into contact with the symptoms of anxiety. You might even absorb stress that isn't your own. Anxiety and stress are both contagious emotions. (If you ever felt like you were walking on eggshells around someone, you were probably picking up on their stress.)

Most important, it does not matter whether you label your symptoms as those of stress or anxiety. In fact, labels can get in the way of your ability to receive the gifts your anxiety offers you. Instead, you will learn how to focus your attention on your specific symptoms—determining where they reside in your body and the information they have to offer. As you learn the ins and outs of each symptom on its own, your confidence in your ability to know what your body is communicating will win out. You begin to look at the *process* instead of the *outcome*. This change of mindset becomes your strongest navigation system toward the gifts.

CHAPTER 2

COMMON CHARACTERISTICS OF ANXIETY

"We can't solve problems by using the same kind of thinking we used when we created them."

—COMMONLY ATTRIBUTED TO ALBERT EINSTEIN

Your Earliest Encounters with Anxiety

Before reading this chapter, close your eyes and take a deep breath. A relaxing, cleansing breath can help you center yourself and prepare to learn more about anxiety.

Anxiety is a conditioned response with roots that extend further than you can imagine. For many, anxiety is a habitual way of reacting to the world. It is a set of mental patterns, memories, bodily responses, attachments, and energetic patterns. Chapter 1 briefly mentioned the basic characteristics and symptoms of anxiety. This chapter goes beneath the surface of those symptoms into some of the conscious and unconscious patterns that drive your thoughts, behaviors, and reactions.

You probably don't remember your first encounters with anxiety—they might have happened as early as in the womb or at the moment of conception. Within eight weeks of conception, your organs were growing rapidly and by week twelve, your nervous system was already communicating messages. Although you did not have the language or experience level to interpret and understand the messages of anxiety, it is likely that you sensed or felt them. Luckily, the womb provided the comfort, protection, and nourishment you needed to deal with those anxious moments.

Once out of the womb, your exposure and experiences with anxiety widened. As a child, you may have learned to imitate responses to stress. Whether the stress was real or imagined does not matter; your body responded as if it were all real. Children are gifted with an imagination and regularly re-enact stressful experiences when they play, such as a dramatic firefighter rescue with trucks and figurines, or parent-child squabbles when "playing house."

Many of the belief systems that feed your current reactions to anxiety were adopted before age six, long before your brain and body were fully developed. What you believed to be true about anxiety was modeled to you through a childhood lens. Some of these are conscious, meaning within your awareness, while others are not. For example:

- The belief that anxiety is bad or a sign of inadequacy may be conscious.
- An unconscious belief, one that you may not be aware of, is the belief that without anxiety you may not survive. This may sound extreme, but many people's relationship with anxiety has been a foundation of their personality. If things don't feel difficult, then something seems wrong.

Mistakenly, you may have been taught to "give away" your energy to help others who are feeling symptoms of anxiety. For example, when children sense something is wrong around them—let's say a parent or teacher is angry about something—they are asked to quiet down or stop what they are doing. As they do, energy leaves their body, meaning they become less aware and connected to what is happening inside and more focused on what they can do (or not do) on the outside. Parents can instead support their children by helping them to identify the difference between losing energy and gaining it. Children learn best from hands-on or visual experience. For example, ask them to imagine a bathtub is draining and explain that's what it feels like to *lose* energy. On the other hand, picturing themselves relaxing in a warm bubble bath may give them an idea of what it feels like to *gain* it. Without engaging in such dialogue, children may unconsciously train themselves and their nervous systems to believe that anxiety is something to be afraid of. When left unattended and unrecognized, these seemingly harmless reactions may become the basis for your adult responses to common anxiety symptoms like those in this chapter.

Ruminating

When you are anxiety focused, you might find yourself experiencing:

- Preoccupations with thoughts
- Worries
- Concerns about the future or relationships
- Shallow breathing and tension
- And many more

Individuals who experience this symptom often report feeling:

- Unable to concentrate
- Frustrated
- "Stuck" or rushed
- Disconnected from their creativity

As much as these symptoms seem like they are a part of you, **anxiety is not who you are.** If you remain loyal to this way of thinking, you make your symptoms the centerpiece of your being.

Anxiety Focused: Overusing Your Brain

Mental chatter can lead to an overuse of the brain. This typically occurs when you don't see your body as a resource. If you break your arm, you are forced to adjust and rely on the opposite arm to go about your day. Making this adjustment requires patience and in most cases will be seen as an inconvenience. The arm that is forced to do all the work may become irritated and sore, while the arm that is resting may weaken. That's what occurs in your brain. Your overused brain becomes "irritated" and your body weakens. When you overuse your brain as a way to solve problems, disregarding your body as a resource, over time your brain becomes strained. This can be recognized by:

- Frustration
- Sensitivity to noise and lights
- Confusion
- Inability to process information in a way that not only makes sense but also anchors you

Truth Focused: Use Your Body As a Resource

What does it mean to "use your body as a resource"? It's the process of redirecting your attention from your thoughts back to your body. Instead of letting your mental chatter gain momentum and run away with itself, you can teach yourself to quiet your mind. Techniques such as breathing methods and meditation (explained further in Chapters 4–6) can help you return to a calmer state, from which you're better able to separate the rational thoughts from the irrational. You will also be able to recognize the difference between actions that are motivated by adrenaline and overstimulated stress hormones and those that are the result of living with your gifts.

Many people don't bother to use their bodies because they think it takes too long, is indulgent, or is a waste of time to meditate or take a moment to breathe deeply. A fast-paced work environment is a common site of such an unfortunate mindset. Yet, constant rumination often makes a job take much longer than it would have if you'd simply quieted your mind for a few moments. Take Sam, for example:

Sam worked as a project manager for a large company for nearly ten years. One of his responsibilities was to come up with innovative ideas to present to consumers. To do this, Sam went through a mental pattern of tossing around ideas in his head, comparing and contrasting each one. This sometimes took days, and during the process he often found himself more and more distracted. Initially this process seemed to work, but over time it began to be less and less productive. The constant rumination caused him to feel further away from his insight, clarity, and intuition. This disconnection left him feeling overworked, exhausted, uncertain, and frustrated.

Sam was overusing his brain and not regarding his body as a resource. Relying on thinking and analyzing things no longer worked. Instead, it increased his stress and frustration levels. This led him to believe that perhaps he had lost his creativity and insight or had grown too old for his chosen field.

Sam's story is not uncommon. Many people have been trained in mental chatter. As you begin to see and utilize your body as a resource, this can change. When the chatter does occur, you will learn that following it only leads to more.

Maryanne experienced a similar journey. She was married with two children. For years, she felt upset about the way her parents overfocused on their problems. Their problems seemed to her to take priority over spending time with their grandchildren. Around them she felt impatient, irritated, and emotionally exhausted. In the past she had attempted to manage these symptoms by ruminating over the problem. This magnified her parents' perceived faults and self-absorbed behaviors, thus creating tension during their visits.

Inside Maryanne knew in order to find peace she needed to find a way to let go of her resentment. She learned how to stay present, breathe, and depersonalize her feelings during a yoga class. To her surprise, she was beginning to learn what "letting go" felt like. In order to let go of the rumination about her parents, she needed to allow it to be a bodily experience. She could choose to accept her parents for who they were, which included their thoughts, behaviors, and decisions. Maryanne had a daily discipline of walking her dog. The walks used to be filled with reviewing events of the past, or listing things to do for the day. But one day, the sights, smells, and sounds around her caught her attention. She felt connected and peaceful.

Finding Faults

Negative or critical self-talk is a key participant in the anxiety cycle. It typically stems from assumptions, judgments, and fears. Fear of criticism and disapproval contribute greatly to the production of negative thoughts. You may recognize it as an inner voice that instead of offering you encouragement, support, and compassion reminds you of everything you are not. Common negative thoughts include:

- They expect me to fail
- I can't
- No one supports me
- I never have enough time

Assuming that you already know what other people will say, think, and believe supports the manifestation of negative thinking. Often it is due to an unconscious belief of inadequacy or drive toward perfection. Ironically, negative self-talk can also be used as a form of self-protection. If you believe you will fail, you might start letting yourself down early to ease the pain. If you tell yourself it won't work out you will be less likely to experience feelings of failure when it doesn't. This can place you at a disadvantage, creating a vicious cycle of wanting things to be different and breeding discontentment, frustration, and inflexibility.

Anxiety Focused: Blaming People, Judging, and Sizing Up Situations

Viewing your anxiety as a problem increases the chances that you may blame or judge the circumstances in your life as the cause of your symptoms. Perhaps your boss, employees, customers, family problems, daily responsibilities, or financial distress occupy your thoughts, causing similar symptoms to resurface.

This prevents you from ever experiencing your gifts. Yet your circumstances are not inherently good or bad—how you choose to view them gives them a negative or positive nature. Instead of judging events, situations, and people, focus on receiving the energy they offer, even if it feels uncomfortable. As you learn how to do this, your perception about your situations will shift. This brings you freedom.

Gift Focused: Learn to Receive

Negative thinking, comparing yourself to others, and finding faults leads you to (consciously or subconsciously) feel as if you need a break or can't catch your breath. When you change your motivation from approval seeking to receiving what your symptoms have to offer, you'll find these responses contribute to the cycle of wanting things to change. This desire may not be something you are consciously aware of; however, the tension and gripping feeling in your body is a fairly good indication that this belief does exist. You may push this idea away, as you have been conditioned to believe a "good" person, mother, father, wife, partner, employee, or student never thinks this way. Instead, tell yourself these symptoms are not about being "good," they are about being real and truthful rather than anxiety focused.

Lucy, the mother of two sons and wife of a husband with diabetes, found that her fault finding, though rooted in hard work, was preventing her from enjoying everyday life. During the day, she worked as a nurse's assistant while attending nursing school part-time. Lucy complained of feeling pulled in many directions. She often found herself feeling guilty for going back to school. When she did have free time, she had trouble enjoying it. Instead, she would fill it up with errands and things she thought she should be doing so she could care for her family. Lucy often talked out loud or to herself. She said things such as: *I can't do anything without my family calling me fifty times, I have to do everything, I feel bad for putting my son in daycare so I can go to school,* and *I feel guilty for taking time for myself.* Lucy had to recognize that the skills and knowledge she learned from her upbringing were contributing to her current mindset. Lucy learned how to *give* and work hard, yet she never had anyone show, model, or tell her how to *receive.* Lucy was able to recognize how the guidance her symptoms had to offer was being blocked by her tendency to find faults. Once she was able to make that connection, she no longer expected others to give her what she longed for. Instead, her symptoms became generators of insight supplementing the development of her gifts.

Instead of Thinking . . .	Lucy Learned to . . .
I have no time for myself	Receive and enjoy the time she does have
I can't do it all	Let go of all-or-none thinking
They think I will fail	Recognize she is already worthy
I feel bad	Release her fear of being judged

Multitasking

Another symptom of anxiety is trying to do a million things at once. Clearly, operating like that on a daily basis requires a lot of energy. Where does that energy come from? Most often, it comes from a misdirected nervous system. Your nervous system is divided into two parts, the sympathetic nervous system and the parasympathetic nervous system. The sympathetic is stimulated when fear or danger is present. When this occurs, blood flow and circulation of nutrients and oxygen become restricted. Your body does this because it believes it is in danger and it needs to protect the vital organs. As blood flow is restricted, energy is depleted from the body.

The parasympathetic nervous system does the opposite. When activated, it stimulates relaxation, circulation, and muscular release, and energy is gained in the body. Your imagination can help you activate this system: Take a moment and close your eyes. Picture a beautiful weeping willow, the sunrise, or endless green fields. Smell and feel the air around you. Imagine your hair blowing gently in a breeze while the warm sun shines on your face. Do this exercise throughout your day, taking a moment to pause and visualize something soothing and beautiful for ten seconds. You could also listen to some peaceful music.

Anxiety Focused: Using False Energy

Anxiety runs off the sympathetic nervous system, which can offer an illusion of productivity. This can take the form of rushing, juggling, and multitasking the events of the day. However, the difference between productivity (gaining energy) and anxiety adrenaline (losing energy) is that the latter typically comes at a cost. When the majority of your energy comes from the sympathetic nervous system, you are more likely to forget important details such as where you put your car keys or appointment times. If you find yourself collapsing from exhaustion at the end of every day, this may also be a sign that anxiety is at play.

Truth Focused: Parachuting

Parachuting your energy is different. Your body is running at full capacity, meaning that rather than your energy being solely directed by your nervous system, it also is being guided by the embodiment of your soul. Imagine what it might be like parachuting in the sky. You may feel a blend of being open, energized, focused, and yet expansive at the same time. Yes, you may feel moments of trepidation, but envision yourself surrendering to this fear, allowing the gentle force of gravity to pull you closer to the earth. Notice where you feel the transition deep in your abdomen and how it shifts to the soles of your feet as your feet touch the ground and land on the earth.

The idea of parachuting energy may seem terrific, but how do you access it? Your breath is one of the greatest ways you can maintain a state of parachuting. (Chapters 4–6 will show you how.) As you learn breathing techniques, you will begin to go about your day noticing small fluctuations in your energy levels. Tasks that may typically worry you or weigh on your mind—such as attending a social event, taking an exam, communicating with your significant other, or working on a computer—become barometers of your energy levels rather than obstacles.

As you learn to parachute, you will be more likely to:

- Live in the moment
- Sense and feel your authentic power
- Both ask for and accept help from others
- Delegate tasks
- Become organized
- Take the time to learn
- Embrace the rising and falling of your energy

Actions such as these preserve energy as well as your awareness of how it is both increased and decreased in the body. Instead of defaulting to sympathetic energy, you can elevate yourself to parachuting energy:

Low-Energy Signals	Parachuting
Talking	Listening
Fixing	Observing
Rushing	Creating
Reacting	Communicating

Parachuting can be especially helpful in social situations. For example, when Jamie was asked by a group of coworkers to go out to dinner, she initially felt excited. As the evening drew closer, however, her sympathetic energy took over and she started to think about the discomfort she may feel since she barely knew the group of people. What would she say? What if they judged her for being so quiet and nervous? One hour before the dinner, Jamie made up an excuse and didn't go.

After working on her parachuting skills, Jamie eventually did join the group on another occasion. What helped her overcome her worrying about what others would think of her was changing her behavior at work. Instead of being solely focused on multi-tasking and getting things done, she made a point to slow down and connect with coworkers a few times during the day. She found the more she did this, the more comfortable she became.

Shutting Down

Some individuals respond to anxiety by shutting down. They withdraw, choosing not to participate in their own lives. They both unconsciously and consciously put blinders on, choosing not to acknowledge or discuss the breakdowns that may be occurring around them. This may be evident in their relationships, work performance, or in their emotional and physical condition. This can go on for months, years, and, in some cases, a lifetime.

Anxiety Focused: Ignoring the Real Message

The consequences of shutting down can be devastating. Divorce, loss of employment, and disease are a few. This is most common in individuals who have been living with the symptoms of anxiety for a long period of time. The symptoms are intended to get your attention, to help you rather than block you from changing your course of action. Individuals who are unaware of this may disregard the message, instead choosing to ignore the symptoms or blame them on something else. This "something else" is often themselves—meaning, somehow everything that has occurred in their lives is all their fault.

Loved ones may react to individuals who shut down by reverting to unwanted criticism, gossip, sharp demands, pressures, and even threats. As a result, a case of the "If onlys" may spread throughout households, threading easily into thoughts and conversations: *If only they could be more this, do that, or change this everything could be better.*

Shutting down or withdrawing is often a form of self-security, a wall of armor that protects you from pain. Unfortunately, what also gets shielded is the ability to feel and know truth. One of the hardest truths is the realization that you have lost yourself—and perhaps worse yet, that you never really knew yourself in the first place. Anxiety was likely something you saw as a weakness rather than as a guidance system. Truly knowing yourself is so much more than identifying your likes and dislikes. It is also understanding your essence, how energy disperses and moves through you, what it feels like to sense purpose, forgive, be silent, and open your heart.

Attempting to force individuals who have shut down to change rarely works. Often, it only makes things worse. For example, after sixteen years of marriage Margaret handed her partner Mathew divorce papers. She had attempted to work with a therapist, but felt that she had no other choice as Mathew "did not want to do the work." She stated that he was quiet, spent the majority of his time working long hours, and did not show any interest in making things better. For some individuals, divorce is indeed the best, and in some cases, the necessary, option. However, one of the messages of anxiety is to teach you about your soul. The soul relates to *feeling* rather than *doing*. Yes, relationships do require skill development and effort—however, love does not. Love is an energy that you can experience yourself and put out to those around you.

Words and energy can sometimes be in conflict. A person can tell you that he wants to remain in a relationship, but his energy might say something different. Some individuals may appear to be resistant, when in fact they may be picking up on the doubt and fears your energy is sending out. Replacing frustrating thoughts about "work" with loving energy will help you move in a more productive direction.

Truth Focused: Feel Your Feelings

Shutting down may relieve the symptoms of anxiety—but only temporarily. Body language and behavior patterns such as fiddling with your phone, watching television, or abusing alcohol create misinformation and poor communication between you and your symptoms. If your senses are dull, it is like taking a long trip—yet when you finally arrive, you never get out of the car. You go through the stress of getting there, without allowing yourself to experience the reward. You have to truly accept and respect your emotions and feelings, rather than pushing them deeper inside you. I witnessed shutting down firsthand one day when I went out to eat with my three daughters. There was a newspaper left on the table. My oldest daughter picked it up and started to read an article. Afterward she said, "Mom, I think you ought to see this." The article was about people getting arrested for child abuse. I read it and put it aside, choosing to focus on what we would order for lunch. As we surfed the menu, I watched the energy of my thirteen-year-old shrink. Previous to reading the article, she was excited about going out to lunch. Now, she sat before me with her shoulders hunched and a look of disgust on her face. When she went to order, she said, "I will get a cup of soup. I am not really hungry." She looked as if something just sucked the life force right out of her. It was apparent to me that she had absorbed the energy from the article.

That experience showed me how certain energy can blindside you into unwanted emotional states, such as fear and depression. Shutting down occurs when energy is retracted and held close to the body in fear. Later I explained to my daughter how you may not always agree, like, or be in alignment with what you see, hear, and feel. However, to maintain resiliency it is important to respect the energy that shows up. "Respecting the energy" means to be attentive to what you feel inside rather than the item or situation that triggered it. Many people disrespect their energy by overfocusing on the trigger. This makes fear grow. Instead, bring your attention to where the energy landed in your body and breathe slowly. Imagine going to hear someone you highly respect speak— perhaps the president, a famous author, or a coworker or friend. If this person were speaking about something painful or traumatic, you might show your respect for this person by listening attentively and giving your full attention to the speech. That's what you want to do to your energy.

On a universal level, the newspaper article was an opportunity to feel the emotions of sadness and anger that perhaps already existed somewhere inside her. To help her connect to her gifts on a broader level, I suggested she consider that the universe provided an opportunity for her to experience emotions like fear, anger, and sadness that may have already been resting inside her. This article served as a bit of a jolt to get her to wake up and attend to these emotions.

Situations such as these remind us of how easily we can pick up energy. The less afraid you are of your symptoms, the less often this will happen. How you choose to utilize your attention will eventually insulate you from being overwhelmed or zapped by your symptoms.

Oh, My Aching . . .

If the symptoms of anxiety are chronically ignored, they may begin to manifest as inflammation or "itis"—in other words, aches and pains. Tension and discomfort often shows up in your neck, back, and jaw. Since stress breaks down the immune system, decreasing blood flow while weakening vital organs such as the heart, it is not uncommon for diseases such as arthritis and gastritis to develop. On March 27, 2014, the *New York Times* published an article called "Stress and Anxiety." The article spoke to the inflammatory response, stating, "Some evidence suggests that chronic stress triggers an overproduction of certain immune factors called cytokines. Such findings may partly explain the association between chronic stress and numerous diseases, including heart disease and asthma."

Health imbalances are one of the louder voices of anxiety. How it manifests is unique to everyone. For many it is through a chronic, nagging pain. Over time individuals living with pain begin to identify it as a part of who they are. At first it may have been related to specific situations, perhaps a family crisis, stress, conflict, or financial hardship—all of which can be, well, a pain. Over time, the mental stress develops into physical discomfort.

That's your body's way of announcing a problem so it can be heard, recognized, and most of all honored.

Aches and pains caused by anxiety are like splinters. At times, the splinter may not bother you, making it tempting to not address it. After all, it can be painful to remove a splinter—just like it can be unpleasant to face a difficult emotion. Eventually old emotions, ones that may have been repressed in the body, grow around the splinter like new skin. Yet the splinter is still in there, causing intermittent pain. This pain is a reminder to pay attention and embrace the sensations you're feeling. No matter how much you want to ignore it, you have to deal with the splinter in order to be truly pain free. The same is true with your emotions. Your emotions have a history, are significant, and are worth paying attention to. With the proper tools and guidance, you can remove the "splinter" and your body can continue healing itself.

Back pain is a common location for displaced anxiety. For example, Jim worked long hours and as a result arrived home exhausted. His wife looked forward to him coming home as she too was looking forward to a break from the daily tasks of raising small children. At work, Jim managed his symptoms of anxiety by keeping busy. However, once home this tactic was no longer effective. Instead, he found himself being impatient and easily frustrated with his wife and children. Impatience and frustration were two emotions he visited frequently. Over time, Jim started to complain of back pain. He typically would try to get rid of it by taking ibuprofen. Later Jim discovered that some of his pain wasn't directly related to parenting but more so due to his longing to have a life without stress. The stress, demands, and responsibility of taking care of the physical, emotional, and financial well-being of others had taken its toll. In fact, he often felt guilty about the way he was quick to snap at the people he loved. The back pain then became a signal that he had been burying emotions. Once acknowledged and honored, the back pain eventually dissipated and he could see the avenues for a more balanced life. Knowing that there were gifts in store for him became his motivation to practice some of the techniques you will learn in Chapters 4–6.

Attachment to "Moving On"

Anxiety, known as a thinking disease, is characterized by overwhelming thoughts. Yet, your thoughts are not the problem—it is the attachment you have to trying to solve whatever comes up in the moment strictly through your intellect that doesn't serve you well. By doing so, you are likely to trigger responses that are based more on past rather than present experiences. B.K.S. Iyengar, author of *Light on Life*, states, "When feelings get anchored by thought into our memory, they become emotions, which are no longer related to the moment but to the past. They accrue a greater density and darkness, like storm clouds that block out the sun itself." Attachments prevent emotions from evolving into something greater—such as your gifts.

Anxiety Focused: Not Allowing Your Emotions to Develop

Attachments come in the form of judgment, assumptions, pressure, and expectations. These responses are observation inhibitors. Your willingness to observe yourself in the moment is one of the most self-loving abilities you could acquire. Chapters 4–6 show you how to allow your thoughts to fully develop into an emotion. When you stop yourself from doing that, it is similar to cutting a perennial flower before it has matured. The nutrients never really get a chance to move back into the root system to nourish the bulb for the following year. This increases stress on the plant, risking its ability to regenerate and survive the years to come. When your emotions are not allowed to assemble fully, your body and brain learn to memorize the discomfort of the symptoms of anxiety rather than the freedom that breathes within them. Attachments are experience blockers. They dull your senses and, like Velcro, connect your energy and attention to expectations and outcome.

Truth Focused: Be Self-Observant

Self-observation is one of the ways to heal and peel away at the barriers that prevent you from claiming your gifts. Attachments come in all shapes and sizes. Rather than attempting to figure out whether you are attached, consider noticing instead whether you are in a state of feeling or nonfeeling. If you are accustomed to functioning predominately from your thoughts, never really allowing them to progress into a feeling, the skills offered to you in Chapters 4–6 will help. As you practice those skills, you will come to realize how expansive your emotions are—and how they connect you to your gifts.

Tina was a single mother who worked as a hairdresser. Sometimes her business was steady and profitable, but other times, it was not. Whenever Tina would have a slow week, her symptoms of anxiety would worsen. She would become fearful, nervous, and irrational in her thinking. She would imagine her business coming to an end, the economy failing, and her being unable to provide for her children. Tina's feelings came from thoughts that brought feelings of doom and gloom. Her wide eyes, tense muscles, and preoccupation with thinking kept her symptoms alive. It was not until Tina and I met that she was able to make a connection between how current thinking both triggered and anchored fears from her past. Some of these fears included the belief that she would not survive as well as deep-seated shame.

When fear is locked up inside of you, have a qualified professional walk you through the process of feeling. Once these past beliefs are set free, the very same symptoms once feared become a source of empowerment. I encouraged Tina to make some small changes in her life. For example:

- Consider listening to lighter, more uplifting music
- Give her fear a color, visualize it as a string, and picture herself cutting it to release it

These changes allowed Tina to feel her fears and let them go.

Dropping Energy

If you place coins in a pocket with holes, you will find yourself dropping coins without even realizing it. A pocket once weighted by pennies and dimes eventually empties into nothing. The workings of anxiety run in a similar way. Instead of dropping coins, however, you drop energy, leaving it in different places and people throughout the day. Perhaps you can recall having a conversation with someone while your attention was somewhere else. If you are in a hurry or behind schedule, you may take a moment to say hello, but quickly find your energy running ahead to the next task.

Meghan found herself in this situation frequently. No matter what time she woke up in the morning, she always found herself running out the door in a panic. This caused her to leave feeling like she forgot something or that she was likely to be late. The dropping-energy analogy hit home with her. While working with Meghan, I asked her to visualize herself dropping coins out of her pockets during the course of her morning. She pictured pennies, dimes, nickels, and quarters spilling out of her pockets as she got ready. By the time she got in the car, her pockets were empty. I then asked Meghan to imagine what it would be like to begin her day with her pockets full. She said, "I would be able to breathe, enjoy the moment, and appreciate the day." To help Meghan fill up her pockets, I asked her to identify the point in her morning when her mind starts rushing. She thought it might be just after she ate breakfast. The one thing she consistently told herself after breakfast was, *I better hurry up, it's getting late.* Rather than *I better hurry up, it's getting late,* I suggested she say silently or out loud, *Thank you for this day.* This simple statement also helped her remember a time when she felt peaceful or grateful (she recalled a place she liked to go for walks). I suggested she place a picture of that place on her bathroom mirror as a reminder to give thanks and to reinforce this feeling in her body during a time when it felt absent. Meghan did this, along with some of the other exercises I suggested (e.g., breathing exercises), for a few weeks and found that changing this habit helped clear her head. She was able to center herself and maintain her energy instead of dropping it.

Anxiety Focused: Leaking Energy

Anxiety happens when you misdirect your energy. Often it is sent away unconsciously by your thoughts. Feelings bring it back into the body. Dropping energy in the past or propelling it into the future are ways that anxiety maintains itself. Since your energy isn't running along with your body, you always feel rushed and "behind schedule." You're not allowing yourself to live in the moment.

Truth Focused: Reclaim Your Energy

Since the gifts are found in the present moment, it will be important for you to learn how to reclaim your energy. To do this, you first need to notice when your energy has escaped you. Eavesdropping on a conversation and leaking energy feel similar: Your physical body is in one place, but your awareness and attention is in another. As a result, your breathing becomes shallow as your thoughts increase. The following Gift Tag is one way to build yourself back up.

Gift Tag

Skill: Crossing Off

Lists are great for people who are experiencing symptoms of anxiety. They stimulate organization, motivation, and clarity. There is something very satisfying about crossing off an item on your list. You might feel a sense of accomplishment or freedom, even if it is temporary. Take a moment to imagine you are making a list of all the comments and words you might say to yourself that force you to drop energy. For example, *I better, I have to, I need to, I better not forget, Oh, crap I forgot*, and more. Visualize or even write down those statements. Now, imagine yourself crossing them off, indicating that you are done with them.

Take a moment and notice how it feels to cross off those statements. Recognize how much you might have relied on them to get you through your day. Perhaps you feel a bit uncertain or lost for words. If so, close your eyes and sit with this energy. You do not have to do anything; simply sit with these uncomfortable feelings. This is the energy that has been running your day. Allow it a minute or two to bubble up inside you and dissipate. Tune into it with your breath. Now, open your eyes and ask yourself, *What would be a more loving way to remind myself of the things on my list?* You may consider adding "breathe" to your everyday to-do lists. Your list might look something like: Oil change, Breathe, Groceries, Breathe, Pick up dry cleaning, Breathe, etc.

CHAPTER 3

WHAT ANXIETY WANTS YOU TO KNOW

"Painful emotions show you what prevents you from creating harmony, cooperation, sharing and reverence for life."

—GARY ZUKAV

The Symptoms of Anxiety Announce Your Needs

Anxiety and its symptoms have something to teach you about your brain, body, conscious, subconscious, and spirit. When you understand how your beliefs, attachments, and attention impact what you receive, you can begin to appreciate the power you have over your own perceptions and growth. Your symptoms are here to serve you. They are not a burden; they are a roadmap to your gifts and a tremendous source of insight into your soul. Any concerns or fears you have about anxiety will be replaced by a motivation to experience your symptoms, as they show up, and then place your attention on both acquiring and appreciating the gifts.

Anxiety and its symptoms inform you of what you need. You may hear yourself say, *I need more time, balance, and support.* You might also experience a deep yearning for a sense of belonging, value, or connection. Without awareness of these messages, you may confuse symptoms such as chronic thinking as feelings. If you quickly react to symptoms before you think about what they might be telling you, you're missing the important messages. Reacting like that is much like a roller-coaster ride. Just when you think it is over, it is followed by emotional spins of disappointment, self-criticism, and frustration. This triggers more thinking and reacting, and before you know it, you are stuffed with an overflow of negative emotions.

The focus on thinking that's prevalent in anxiety blocks you from experiencing your symptoms. This thinking masks what your symptoms (when experienced) have to offer, your gifts. Think of it like a game show that has three curtains and you are supposed to guess which one has the prize behind it. You try really hard to think about which one to pick. Using that method, you might hear yourself say, *I better get this right* or *I will be so upset if it is the wrong one.* As a result you may feel nervous, doubtful, and scared.

Or you could try closing your eyes, taking a deep breath, and feeling and sensing the answer. You may even feel it in your gut or tell yourself, *I know which one it is.* Your gifts work in a similar way—they come from feeling rather than thinking. The following table shows you the difference in the two approaches.

Intellectualizing/Thinking	Sensing
Act first, then feel	Feel first, then act
What If	What Is
Project doubt and fear	Tap into what you know
Tighten your body	Relax your body
Come from missing energy	Come from having energy

Stefanie found that her anxiety brought messages that she had approached with thoughts instead of feelings. When Stefanie came to me as a client, I asked her what her passion was. She said she loved to paint but had not in a long time due to the fact that she was always caring for everyone else. Stefanie was an only child, and her father had died when she was six years old. Although she had many extended family members who helped her mom raise her, unconsciously she had suppressed the deep loss and sadness she felt over her father's death. Through our work together, she realized a great deal of her energy as a child, adolescent, and into adulthood was spent on comforting others. Even if she was not comforting them physically or with words, she did this through her energy.

For example, she recalled a time when she was eight playing with a friend and thinking her mom would be home and she should go be with her. Although she enjoyed her friend, her energy was not present. She had projected it into the future, thinking she should be with her mother. This may seem like a loving thing to do. However, this pattern continued throughout her lifetime. When she would sit down to paint, she once again sent her energy into the future, wondering if her husband needed her. Then she'd put off painting for another time. Eventually she created her own barriers, cluttering her art space with miscellaneous items and unfinished projects, making it seem impossible for her to work.

Through meditation, energy training, and spiritual counseling, I taught Stefanie about the gifts and how to access them. Much of the time was spent allowing suppressed feelings to rise to the surface, where they could be healed. By the sixth session, Stefanie had cleaned off her workspace and was painting freely. She was aware of how sending her energy away blocked her from her peace and potential. She was able to recognize how shutting down her energy actually disconnected her from her deceased loved ones. Her years of giving away her energy had left her feeling alone, anxious, and disconnected from her gifts.

Allowing herself to explore her symptoms also transformed her art. It became not only an expression but a direct route to her gifts. She would imagine her paintbrush breathing, inhaling and exhaling, across the canvas. By interacting with her painting in this way she gave it life and restored her own body from the loss it once carried. Now her paintings carry this energy, making it possible for others to receive the gifts she has to offer.

Stefanie's experience illustrates how fear, the undercurrent of anxiety, can be transformed into a deeper understanding of self. By redirecting her energy inward, Stefanie was able to loosen her tendencies to react rather than feel her emotions.

Anxiety is like a fever. It's a sign that there's something going on beneath the surface—something that needs attention. There are times when the symptoms are intense and strong while other times they can be subtle, barely noticeable. Part of the process of discovering your gifts is to notice and learn what your symptoms are trying to tell you. That's what this chapter is all about.

Learn to Receive

If someone asked you if you knew how to give, your response may be automatic. You may get a picture in your mind, such as a dollar sign to represent giving your money away, or lending someone a hand with a yard project, or a wrapped birthday present. Your connection to giving may be ingrained into your system from years of conditioning. Most likely, your brain has stored giving as an act you do for someone else—a way to show love, support, concern, or attention. Of course, there's nothing wrong with that type of giving.

Giving can go a step too far if you unconsciously learned to give your *energy* away.

Bottling Up Emotions Separates You from Your Gifts

If you are experiencing anxiety, you may be quite adept at giving away your energy. When giving takes precedence over receiving, you overshadow the benefits of giving to yourself and deprive yourself of experiencing the graceful energy that receiving brings. Giving away your energy is a way to prevent others from feeling bad—something children are very attuned to. In fact, these types of behaviors and beliefs were often created before you were given the words or had the ability to understand what was happening around you. Instead, children function more off instinct. They sense when things feel calm, open, and loving and when their environment is fearful or unsafe. One of the ways they sense this is through energy. Anxiety and its symptoms can trigger emotions that have been lodged inside your body. Think about it: your emotions are tied into how well you remember things. The more emotionally charged an event is, the more likely you are to recall it later. Even when your brain cannot recall something, your body is likely to keep the memory of certain emotions alive. Without realizing it you may have memories of anger, pain, and fear recorded inside you. Inadvertently, as a way to manage and protect itself from experiencing emotional pain, you may have developed an invisible energetic wall around your heart.

Dr. Bradley Nelson, author of *The Emotion Code*, refers to this wall as a heart wall. It's a wall made of emotions (energy) that were too intense to experience or were not permitted to be experienced for one reason or another. For example, maybe your parents didn't like it when you cried as a child—so instead of expressing sadness, you tucked away that emotion inside. Or maybe other kids teased you for being afraid, so instead of showing your fear, you bottled it up inside. This energy thus becomes trapped inside the body. Individuals with protective energetic layers may find it more difficult to connect to, express, and release their feelings.

Part of the process of learning how to receive includes identifying and accepting without judgment the emotions and beliefs that may be caught inside your body. For example, some individuals who have lived with anxiety symptoms for a long period of time claim they "do not feel anything." It is through their behavior or health that they notice something inside may be off. For example, they might feel cynical, over-reactive, or numb. They might have trouble sitting still, long for a different way of life, or have difficulty enjoying the present moment. Their energy is either pushed away or kept at arm's length, never really allowed it to touch them in any way. The energetic wall built up around them makes it difficult for them to develop trust or deepen their relationships. This may be due to a subconscious fear of experiencing their own emotions or a belief that it will only create more pain and suffering.

Go with the Flow

If a plant was dry and you gave it water, it would begin to flourish and grow. However, if you give it too much water, flooding its roots, you don't allow it to absorb, adapt, and receive the nourishment. As a result, it may become weak and even possibly die from being overwatered. A state of flow is creating inner balance through self-observation. If you notice your energy is dry, water it with your awareness, digest it with your breath, and tend to it with your intentions. A state of flow is fostered by the connection between mind, body, and spirit. There will be times when energy moves swiftly through you, coupled with moments where you will benefit from it resting softly inside you. There are days when you will find yourself motivated and moving through your day with ease, while other days, you may need to take a nap, sit down, and do nothing. Flow is strengthened when you give yourself time to fill up as well as opportunities to release energy that has been built up inside you. Living from flow and nonflow take on very different outlooks:

Flow

- You are able to experience all of your emotions freely, without becoming swept up in the stories or experiences they carry.
- During challenging times, higher emotions (appreciation) pull you through.
- You are able to experience emotions such as joy, peace, and love more deeply.
- You are able to take breaks and place boundaries in your life without beating yourself up.

Nonflow

- You overfocus at times, obsessing over the thoughts and stories your emotions carry.
- During challenging times, you tend to revert to lower emotions (e.g., frustration, anger) to pull you through.
- Your experiences with emotions such as appreciation are brief.
- You view rest, boundaries, and breaks as a sign that there is something wrong with you.

When you give to others from a state of nonflow, everything feels like work. This eventually breeds resentment toward others, whether conscious or subconscious. Anxiety is a signal that you're experiencing an imbalance of energy flow. The process of flow is intricate and quite miraculous. So many systems are at work. Keep in mind, energy runs through each and every organ, muscle, gland, and cell. Avoid being quick to assume that something is wrong when you feel the need to slow down and retreat. It could be that a lower emotion such as fear is attempting to clear itself, and your body needs a bit of time to digest and reorient itself. Most people have been conditioned to believe that giving to others takes precedence, even if it comes at a cost to them energetically. Studies show that volunteer work can decrease stress and anxiety in both the giver and the receiver. This is because it opens your heart. However, if you are helping others out of guilt or obligation, ignoring your bodily feedback, you risk the chance of depleting your own energy as well as theirs. Remember, anxiety is contagious. No one knows that better than Jill Bolte Taylor. In the book *My Stroke of Insight*, she describes her recovery from a stroke. She began to notice the people that helped her heal—as well as those who did not. Individuals who walked into her hospital room consciously and lovingly, meaning they moved and spoke more slowly, gave her energy. On the other hand, those who seemed to visit out of obligation brought nervous energy that depleted her. She learned to protect herself from individuals who might take her energy. As author Maya Angelou said, "I've learned that people will forget what you said, people will forget what you did, but people will never forget how you made them feel." Once you can receive your own feelings first, you are able to give positive energy to those around you.

Receive Your Feelings

Beliefs come in all shapes and sizes. If you carry the belief that it is bad to feel, it can be difficult to create healthy relationships with yourself or others. Since the self is made up of mind, body, and spirit, this includes a relationship with your higher consciousness, the part of you that contains insight, wisdom, and unconditional love.

Receiving is feeling. Anxiety and its symptoms serve as a reminder to feel, rather than think.

If you resonate with the statement *I cannot feel*, or *feeling is wrong*, or *feeling is a sign of weakness*, the following exercise (as well as the guidance in Chapters 4–6) will help you.

Exercise: Release Your Resistance to Feel

Sit in a chair. Close your eyes and make sure your feet are resting on the floor. Imagine the warm sun shining down upon you. Allow this feeling to travel down your head, neck, around your shoulders, to your arms, torso, and into your hips, then all the way down into your toes. Imagine this warm sun scanning over different parts of your body for ninety seconds. Relax your face and jaw, separating your lips and allowing your shoulders to fall away from your earlobes.

Now, consciously state and name the belief, *I cannot feel* or *feeling is hard for me*. (You may say it out loud or silently.) Hear your own voice state the words and bring the thought to the forefront of your mind.

Next, give your heart, mind, body, and soul permission to release this belief. Imagine it rolling down the back and front of your head, face, neck, down your spine, off your sacrum, down the back and front of your legs and feet. See this energy rolling off you like a warm shower. Know your intention, presence, and willingness to release this belief are enough.

Gift Tag

Exercise: Receiving Ritual

Try this quick and easy ritual to practice receiving. First, identify moments when you go outside regularly. For example, it may be getting your mail, walking your dog, or getting into your car. At those times, take a moment and receive the air, temperature, and sounds around you. Imagine the wind returning the energy that you scattered throughout the day. Hear the rustling of the leaves, birds chirping, rain, or snow—those could also symbolize this returning of energy. Take a deep breath in, signaling to your body that you receive the energy. Then take a long exhale, and imagine this returned energy circulating and nourishing your body.

Choose Resiliency

Self-esteem is often associated with a perfect woman with flawless skin, wearing flattering clothes and smiling on a beautiful day. Never do you associate self-esteem with an image of yourself sitting around with your hair tied up, coffee stains on your shirt, reading a gripping novel. Anxiety wants to help you rethink this beautification of self-esteem. It does so by attempting to give you a true understanding of the difference between self-esteem and resiliency.

What's the Difference Between Self-Esteem and Resiliency?

Have you ever noticed that your levels of self-esteem tend to vary depending on the situation or task at hand? Not to worry, this is normal. Self-esteem is when you feel competent and capable—but it's impossible to feel a sense of competency in *every* situation. Therefore, not only is self-esteem meant to go up and down, but it is actually necessary so that you are motivated to learn something new or create change.

Resiliency is a bit different. It runs like a pilot flame; it is always there. However, how resilient you are is not about whether you have the pilot flame, but how well you maintain it. Do you attend to your flame by tuning into your energy? Are you aware of influences that may weaken it? What habits and rituals do you already have in place to support it? For example, do you allow yourself to take a deep breath? If so, do you take a moment to notice and fully absorb the sensations that accompany it?

Quite often, both resiliency and self-esteem are reflected in your attitude. The more resilient you are, the more likely you are to imagine yourself being able to move through any perceived obstacles. In fact, resilient people are less likely to view challenges as obstacles—instead, they use them as a guidepost for setting the pace for the process. Resiliency is about trust, a sense of certainty that the universe is on your side and always has your greater interests in mind. Rather than seeing things as working against you, you assume they are all happening for you.

The following table shows how self-esteem and resiliency go hand in hand.

Self-Esteem	Resiliency
Positive appraisal of self	Belief in your ability to get through life's challenges
Strong, confident body language (e.g., eye contact)	Faith in your values and beliefs
Able to speak up (verbally) for self	Emotionally aware
Feel a sense of competency	Able to see the competency and capability of others
Utilizes positive self-talk (such as *I am capable*)	Appreciates the value and contribution of others
Strives for mastery	Views mistakes as choices
Acceptance of who you are	Acceptance of the energy you are experiencing
Able to identify your tools/resources	Able to embody tools/resources

As we've discussed, the symptoms of anxiety provide you with a gauge of how much of your energy is from thinking and how much is from feeling. Feelings of preoccupation, worry, doubt, or fear will suppress your resiliency. However, if you are hopeful, forgiving, and able to make mistakes without treating yourself poorly, you strengthen your resiliency.

The Connections Between Self-Esteem and Resiliency

In my opinion maintaining resiliency fosters self-esteem. I believe we come into this world already resilient. After all, children are some of the most resilient people on the planet. The more in tune you are with your energy, the more likely you are to cultivate it in a way that allows you to witness your inner light and strength—and resiliency—no matter what the situation. Resiliency is about respecting your energy. Energy represents your life force, and through skill development and practice it can be fostered in a way that benefits you. As this occurs, you increase your potential to positively influence others. If you don't respect your emotional energy—if you direct it in a way that separates your mind, body, and spirit instead of uniting them—you are minimizing your gifts.

Latesha was a college student who took pride in getting a perfect grade point average. On the outside, she looked like a competent, capable young woman. Yet years of taking honors classes and working a job simultaneously were beginning to take their toll. She started to experience symptoms of trouble sleeping, fear, irritability, and dread of the future. People around her would remind her of how smart and capable she was. Although she knew she was doing well in school, inside, she felt weak and unhappy.

Latesha's anxiety was trying to tell her to respect and experience her emotions instead of pushing past them. During counseling, Latesha was able to recognize that although her stress was about maintaining good grades, a great deal also came from worrying about her family. In fact, her willpower to do well came from a deep-seated desire to have a different life, one that did not come with conflict, fear, and struggle. Through meditation and guided visualization, Latesha learned how to experience her feelings rather than push them away. This renewed her resiliency and showed her how self-esteem is not solely developed from accomplishments. It is also highly connected to your ability to cultivate and maintain energy.

"Finish" Your Feelings

This section is about attachment to being "done." Attachment, as described in Chapter 2, is a state of nonfeeling. Have you ever heard yourself say *I am all done* or *I have had enough*? The symptoms of anxiety want you to know that you are not done. Yes, you may feel "done" with an actual physical experience, such as working at a certain job, engaging in a difficult relationship, or supporting the irresponsible behaviors of others. However, as teacher and workshop presenter Zoe Marae, PhD, suggests, emotionally it is actually likely that you are not done, meaning there is more for you to experience. Though that sounds counterintuitive, try the following eye-opening exercise to see the situation in a new light.

Exercise: Are You Really "Done"?

The next time you hear yourself say *I'm all done*, either silently or aloud, take a moment and assess how you're feeling. The tone of voice you use will show you whether you truly are "done." If your tone of voice is compassionate or delivered with respect, then you may feel a sense of relief from those words, indicating your energy is flowing (and anxiety free). However, if you say these words in a negative, sarcastic, or abrupt tone, your energy may be dense and heavy, indicating nonflow. This mindset invites heavier emotions such as fear, frustration, and anger.

Your gifts are found from flow. That is why it is worthwhile to explore how different types of thoughts and behaviors impact your state of mind. (The skills presented in Chapters 4–6 will show you how.)

Experience Your Emotions from Beginning to End

Although it only takes about ninety seconds to feel an emotion from beginning, to middle, to end, many people store or hold in their emotions, never really giving them a chance to run their course. It is like putting clothes in a washing machine but never allowing them to move through all the cycles of water, soap, rinse, and spin. Or putting shampoo in your hair and never rinsing it out. Sure, you could function wearing wet clothes and walking around with shampoo in your hair . . . but eventually this lifestyle will get old and you'll be chronically uncomfortable.

Opening the Chain

One of the most challenging parts of anxiety is its contagious nature. Just like you might pick up another person's cold, anxiety symptoms can also be absorbed. Picture a single chain link in a room filled with anxious people. Add another link to the chain each time someone in that room absorbs the symptoms from another person, and before you know it you will have a very long chain circling everyone in the room! Just thinking about that image, you probably have an urge to run out of the room. The reality is many of the things and situations that bring about anxiety are unavoidable. For example, each and every child goes through the terrible twos (or threes), and you can't really divorce your parents. Instead, you can learn to gently and intentionally open the chain. Believe me, the rewards are much greater.

You cannot change how someone else feels and the way his symptoms impact his behavior. However, you can influence your resiliency, meaning your ability to repel negative energy. Later in Chapter 11, you will learn how to support others. For now, it is important that you continue to stay committed to your own journey by keeping the focus on you. It is tempting to want to veer off and peer over at others to nitpick at how they are handling the very same symptoms you grapple with. This doesn't make you a bad or competitive person—your mind may be more trained to look at others as a way to gauge or control your own feelings of self-doubt and criticism. If this is so, remember you are not done. There is more for you to experience, and the closer you stick to your own path the more clear your gifts will be.

In order to open the chain, you need to recognize when you are absorbing the energy of someone else's emotions. Individuals who are highly empathetic, sensitive, or intuitive tend to be energy absorbers. Their feelings tend to be one of the driving forces behind their behaviors. Energy absorbers are often found in teaching professions and medical and human services. Employers love individuals with such characteristics, as they are known to go above and beyond the call of duty, at times for little or no pay. However, over time, if continued without awareness and the ability to set boundaries, energy absorption will weaken them. If some of the earlier signs such as tension, irritability, and fatigue are ignored, it is not uncommon for aches, pains, and even disease to set in.

Therefore, it is important to learn the difference between empathizing and caring for others and preventing or carrying the feelings of others. One way to do this is to notice the makeup of your emotional load. Ask yourself, *Am I consuming others' feelings and experiences as my own?* How might I identify this in my thoughts, speech, and actions? Keep in mind, there are no right or wrong answers; there is simply an awareness of how you might be picking up anxiety. Nonetheless, if you are experiencing the symptoms, they are now yours as well.

Here's what that situation might look like. Tom and Sabrina had been married for sixteen years. Over the course of time, Sabrina had gotten into the habit of saying something positive each time Tom said something negative. Initially, she did it to try to brighten up the moment, but over time it became a habitual response. Tom would state something negative perhaps about the weather and Sabrina would quickly negate his response by saying the opposite. This only made Tom feel worse and Sabrina feel exhausted. Unconsciously, Sabrina had given herself the role of picking Tom up, which over time made her feel like she was taking care of another child. Sabrina's growing resentment and fatigue were signs that she was trying to control rather than honor Tom's emotions. Attempting to control other people's feelings makes you more susceptible to absorbing them.

To open the chain, Sabrina would need to break her pattern of behavior. Instead of reacting to Tom's words and statements, she learned how to redirect her attention to her own experience, to how she may be preventing herself from feeling her uneasiness or discomfort through habitual verbal responses. Sabrina began noticing how her body felt when she sensed tension from her husband. By observing her own tension, she could reframe her responses. She may feel the impulse to respond, but instead choose to take a deep inhale (sensing the tension) and exhale (circulating the energy of the emotion). To deepen this practice she could practice the following Gift Tag. Words can either land on you like a ton of bricks or pass by you like the wings of a butterfly. If you feel tightness in your jaw and shoulders, it is likely that you are absorbing the words (energy) of others. The more your energy flows, the less words stick.

Gift Tag

Meditation: Relax Your Mouth

Close your eyes and take a deep belly breath (inflating the belly on inhale and contracting it on exhale). Do this three times, before you begin your day or at some time when you have a quiet moment. On the third breath, loosen your lips and imagine the energy of your breath swirling around your mouth like mouthwash—only instead of mouthwash, it is pure water. This water is not only free of toxins but also contains healing qualities. Perhaps it comes from a spring deep in the mountains.

As you swish the water around in your mouth, pretend that it is filled with vitamins and minerals that cleanse and clear your mind, body, and soul. By allowing the breath to swirl and rinse your mouth, you are experiencing rather than reacting to the muscular energy that moves your tongue. This is the same energy that may cause you to speak quickly or impulsively.

This visualization teaches you how to slow down and experience your energy instead of projecting it or absorbing it from your environment.

Clean Out Your Emotional Backpack

Talking, listening, and learning about anxiety may not exactly be at the top of your "things that are fun to do" list. You may even believe that giving anxiety this kind of attention will only exacerbate the pain and discomfort of memories you do not wish to dig up. These memories could include past hurts, disappointments, anger, heartbreak, and more. Yet you can't release and clear emotions that you aren't acknowledging. Anxiety wants you to be aware of what you have been carrying—anxiety wants you to clean out your emotional backpack.

Cleaning out your emotional backpack is like cleaning out your attic, basement, or garage. Years of accumulation makes the task seem overwhelming, time-consuming, and downright impossible. You may find yourself questioning whether or not it's really a good idea to even try—will it truly help you? Are you really ready? Anxiety says yes to both questions. You are ready because in truth what you believe to be anxiety is really love in disguise. As you approach the four gifts, you will understand more clearly how and why.

Your backpack is overstuffed with unfinished experiences and emotions. (The tools in Chapters 4–6 will provide you with the skills for finishing them.) The good news is, you do not need to completely rehash or dig up the past to clean out your backpack. As you empty your emotional backpack, simply be mindful of experiences that appear negative. It is likely they did serve you in some way. In addition to discovering what is unfinished, anxiety wants you to know there is more for you to receive. As you think about anxiety in a new way, you will learn there is always something to receive. Think of all the individuals you may know who have been through hardship and in the end were able to see a hidden blessing in the experience. For example, someone who loses a job may discover the compassion of family and friends. Perhaps you had an experience that was initially disappointing, like Matt did.

Matt was a hard-working father and husband. His line of work required long hours that went far into the night. The stress was beginning to take its toll on his health. He felt obligated to continue to provide for his children. He knew he needed to make a change, but he was unsure what the change would be. Another parent who owned a similar business heard of the work he did and offered him a job in his company for less pay. Although the pay was much less, the hours and type of work felt right. Matt was incredibly excited about the opportunity. He was just about to accept the offer when he discovered he would need to pay his own health insurance. As a result, he was unable to take the position. This left him feeling frustrated, disappointed, and beaten down. As he reflected on his life, he viewed it as a series of unfair experiences. Yet even in this disappointment, Matt received a gift: the realization that he no longer wished to be self-employed or work at night. He wanted a daytime position, with finite hours and an end to the day.

Matt's perception of his life as a series of unfair experiences may perhaps actually be a series of unfinished emotions. Rather than feel them, he thinks about them. Many people think about their past hurts and disappointments instead of feeling them because they don't know any other way. They were never taught what their emotions were, never mind how to feel them. One of the blessings offered to Matt during the experience was clarity. However, his attachment to his thoughts prevented him from initially perceiving it that way.

Become Aware of Your Subconscious Mind

On average, human beings have approximately 50,000 to 70,000 thoughts per day. You actually experience more thoughts than breaths in one day. Thinking is how you solve problems, remember things, and make decisions. It is what makes you human. The famous philosopher René Descartes said, "I think, therefore I exist." As scientists learn more about what it means to live consciously, however, statements such as these are now debated. Advances in technology have provided unprecedented knowledge about your ever-changing brain. The words, thoughts, and actions you choose play a tremendous role in the development of your personality. You have the ability to strengthen the parts of you that promote tranquility, flexibility, and acceptance. In fact, quantum physicists now report that human beings operate with about 10 percent conscious thought, meaning that a full 90 percent of who you are comes from your subconscious mind.

Mark Waldman, coauthor of *Words Can Change Your Brain*, sees enough evidence to support the movement of conscious living to revise Descartes's quotation from "I think, therefore I am" to "I am, therefore I think." The subconscious mind is the invisible part of self that remembers everything. It turns out you can only be aware of about 10 percent of what is influencing you. The remaining beliefs, memories, and emotions are held in your subconscious mind. Thus, the vast majority of your daily choices, moods, decisions, insights, and ideas originate from the workings of your subconscious mind.

Becoming aware of your subconscious mind places you at an advantage. Through tools and techniques such as meditation and hypnosis, psychologists are discovering you can transform and shape the quality of information that is stored in the subconscious mind. For example, if as a child you were raised by parents who worked a lot, you may have unconsciously picked up the belief that it is wrong to take care of yourself. Later, as an adult, you may have difficulty making time for yourself, become easily distracted, or put others first. This is likely due to the earlier recordings in your subconscious mind.

Chapter 4 also offers you techniques so you can access and reprogram your subconscious mind. This means you can clear the root cause of your symptoms. Clearing and reprogramming your subconscious mind literally gives you a new mind. You can release stories and memories that contain emotions of unworthiness or shame, and make space for stories of courage and love.

Gift Tag

Exercise: I Am More Than This

The next time you feel stuck or overwhelmed by your thoughts, state to yourself out loud or silently, *I am more than this*. Speak to the larger part of who you are. Some people refer to this as their higher self, the part of themselves that speaks from the heart and knows what is best. You are more than the present thoughts you are thinking. Close your eyes and allow yourself to breathe and feel how expansive you are.

You Are Already Complete

Your body is already complete with everything you need to bring balance and harmony to your life. Take a breath—I realize not many of us are used to thinking or hearing that. But it's true: your body specifically and miraculously contains everything you need to steer and steady your mind. There is nothing for you to fix, do, or purchase. Anxiety and its symptoms are your body's way of directing you to what you already have. Therefore, it is not a matter of getting more of something, but rather learning how to tap into what already exists. In order to do so, it is important that you give yourself permission to accept this as true. If you have a belief that you are not enough, you will need to release that belief and reprogram a new one into your system. The Gift Tag in this section will help you.

Your body is truly a miracle. Your body knows how to keep you safe physically, emotionally, and physiologically. For example, if you put your hand on a hot stove, the neurons in your body deliver a message of fear so you remove your hand. It does this by communicating messages between the brain and body via the nervous system, which is located in your spine. Think of it as a communication highway. Billions of neurons circulate your brain and body daily.

In addition to your parasympathetic nervous system (which was discussed in Chapter 2), you have other built-in mechanisms that soothe and quiet your mind and body. These include your:

- Brain's right and left hemisphere working together
- Body's energy levels
- Muscles
- Respiratory system

By engaging just one of these symptoms, you can influence all of them. For example, by taking a long, deep breath, inflating your lungs fully, you circulate oxygen while expelling carbon dioxide. Balancing out your oxygen/carbon dioxide levels shifts your overall mood and attitude. Automatically (without direction from your thoughts), you will experience relief from tension held in your muscles and tissue. Taking a deep, long breath also increases the flow of your energy, while simultaneously activating your brain's right hemisphere, where consciousness is stimulated. The collaboration between these systems produces sensations that slow down brain wave activity while inducing higher states of being, referred to as consciousness. Pretty cool, huh?

That's just one small example of how you were enough and complete with everything you needed the moment you were conceived. In fact, your resources are limitless. See yourself as *having plenty*.

Gift Tag

"I Am Complete" Mantra

Author Deepak Chopra describes mantras as ancient power words that contain subtle intention. Many times they induce a sound or vibration in the body. If you have a belief that you are not enough, consider stating the Sanskrit mantra "So Hum" to yourself nine times, three times per day, for one month. The English translation for "So Hum" is "I am." Repeating this mantra daily will help you reframe the energy of "I am not" into "I am." Your words and thoughts carry a vibration, and with intention and commitment, you can release the energetic bind, thus creating space for new vibrations and beliefs about yourself. In addition, any symptoms of anxiety you are presently experiencing will transform into higher states of mind.

You Can Heal Yourself

Everyone is a healer. Not everyone chooses or is meant to work as one, but anxiety wants you to know that you can heal yourself. In fact, people have been healing themselves for thousands of years. Accounts of medical miracles have been noted, some with unexplainable outcomes. Authors such as Dr. Joe Dispenza are now pulling these accounts together as a way to measure and learn about how and why spontaneous healings take place.

We've discussed the many ways energy may be escaping you. Handling the symptoms of anxiety through behaviors such as eating, gossiping, thinking, or self-imposed pressure is like pouring your energy down the drain. Healing happens when you feel full energy. You are at your fullest when you are fully engaged with the present moment. Contemplate for a moment a time when you felt inspired by an experience, perhaps when you were doing what you love or felt inspired by watching a performance or engaging with a loved one. These moments are significant, as they help your body capture what it feels like to be whole.

Before you can begin to heal yourself from symptoms such as worry, insecurity, or sleeplessness, it is important for you to understand what healing looks and feels like. For people who have dedicated their lives to caring for others, this may seem like a difficult thing to imagine. When it comes to healing yourself, it is less about giving and more about receiving. To do this well, you must loosen any counterproductive fears you have about healing (more on this in Chapter 7). How you handle stress and anxiety often reveals what you believe to be true about vulnerability. For example, if you are a quick responder, meaning you attack every problem by immediately taking action, you may secretly fear the experience of emotions such as uncertainty and sadness. On the other hand, some people procrastinate in dealing with a problem as a way to avoid feeling fear. This tactic may serve you well in some situations; however, left unattended the fear of uncertainty can take its toll on your heart. Left unresolved, it creates space for loss and disappointment.

Allowing yourself to experience the unknown is what restores your faith and gives you the ability to heal yourself. Your anxiety symptoms showed up to teach you this. Your body never meant to trip you up or make you suffer—everything that has happened in your life has been an opportunity for you to dig deeper into the archives of your soul and understand more about yourself.

How you choose to acknowledge and use your energy determines how, when, and if you heal. If you abuse your energy through actions such as sleep deprivation, eating unhealthy foods, negative thinking, and getting little to no exercise this will unfavorably influence your healing potential.

Gift Tag

Reflection: Healing Is Engaging

Anxiety is like a small child or a puppy looking for attention. At first, you might think the child wants you to play with him. After you engage the child in play you might realize that he just wanted you to notice him and be heard. He wanted to share his energy. Children are often bursting with energy because they have so many ideas and creative ways of seeing the world. They can often shift in and out of emotional states easily. One minute they are frustrated, and the next minute they are laughing.

Anxiety wants you to know that this is what healing feels like. It can be messy, loud, quiet, or soft. Try not to put parameters around it. Self-imposed expectations will only get in the way.

Restore Your Faith

Having your faith shaken by the doubt, insecurity, and worry brought upon by the symptoms of anxiety can be enough to put just about anyone out of balance. Certain life events can test your belief in a higher, loving force. Believe it or not, anxiety never wanted you to question your faith. It wanted you to restore it. It does this by nudging you toward your higher self. Your higher self is the part of you that is whole and complete. It is the part of you that says, *I am already enough.*

Many of us never learned about what a higher self was, never mind how to connect to it. Think of your anxiety symptoms as a "disconnected" icon on your cell phone, showing you that you're not connected to the Internet or that you have no phone reception.

To restore your faith, receive the symptoms as a sign that you are temporarily offline. Renew your connection and you will renew your faith. It may not look the same as before—meaning that as you transform, so will your beliefs. For some, your newly restored faith may not be exactly in line with how you were raised. As long as the foundation of what you choose to believe is built on love (not fear), your faith will be rejuvenated.

To have faith means to believe. By releasing the binding influences of your symptoms, you are both alerting and giving your soul permission to support you. This is the part of you that knows and trusts that you are not alone and that everything will be okay. One of the beliefs that interfere with your soul development is the belief that you are at fault. You may feel consciously or unconsciously responsible for the pain and suffering of another or for a specific event in your life. The symptoms of anxiety may exist because they want you to ask that question of yourself: Is there a situation or event in your life that you silently blame yourself for? It could be a divorce, death, loss of job, or breakdown in health. If the answer is yes, let the energy of that belief go so you can restore your faith in yourself.

Holding on to beliefs such as these could be considered a form of self-abuse. It is no different from telling yourself you are fat, ugly, wrong, or bad. It also puts another belief into play: that you are the only one in control, meaning there are no other forces at work. Beating yourself up over a past mistake is a common way that people's faith becomes disconnected. For example, John lost his five-year-old son thirty years ago in a drowning accident. Since John was in charge of watching the boy at the time, he spent the majority of his life blaming and punishing himself for this event. He did this by turning to drugs and engaging in risky behaviors, such as stealing and lying. In many ways, he was looking to get caught so that he would go to prison, which is what he truly believed he deserved. Eventually, John became sober and committed himself to a recovery practice. Although his life went on, he continued to carry the pain and suffering of his son. He was unable to talk about the death and would rarely visit the grave.

It wasn't until John saw a spiritual counselor that he was able to identify some of the beliefs he was carrying. Using some of the tools in Chapters 4–6 of this book, John's faith in something greater strengthened. As he allowed himself to feel his feelings and move his energy, he was able to feel connected to his son. It was then that he was able to accept that his actions that day were a mistake; however, *he* was not a mistake and neither was the life of his son. He was able to recognize that perhaps God did have another plan for his boy. Today he has a strong meditation practice, where he visualizes play with his son. This brings him great peace and joy.

Your Energy Is Perfect

There is something perfect about you, and everyone else on the planet for that matter: your energy. The fact that your energy is a direct connection to your soul makes you flawless. It is your perception that muddles pure energy, tainting it with thoughts, beliefs, and emotions (such as guilt and depression). Energy is meant to be experienced, felt, and tuned into. It is a big part of how you learn to navigate and connect to your world. It connects you not only to your gifts but also to the here and the now—a place where the symptoms of anxiety cannot live. Your energy is perfectly designed to take you there.

Acknowledging the symptoms of anxiety is an act of courage. Many people hide or disregard such opportunities out of fear or shame of what they might see. They hide under a mask of *I'm fine* or judge others who follow such paths as abnormal. Instead they may choose to push through the symptoms as a way to preserve an illusion or desire to be perfect. This may be because they believe the symptoms convey their weaknesses. They worry others will see their screwups, judging them as incapable, unintelligent, unworthy, or lazy. Instead of focusing on what is *right* about them, they fixate on what is *wrong*, not only with themselves but also the world around them.

As you get to know your perfect (energetic) self, your attention will naturally shift from attending to thoughts to noticing what feels right. To do this well, you will need to reshape your perception of the word *right*. Currently, it may be associated with what is "correct." If you change this definition to "what feels well or complete," you will open doors to allowing your emotions to be accepted and respected.

People, things, and accomplishments do not complete you; your perfect energy does. The circumstances in your life highlight the energy that is eager to be brought to completion. Your perfect energy is what makes you and every other living thing on the planet whole. It is how you shine your light on the world.

If you feel unsure, unfamiliar, or disconnected from your perfect energy, the tools in the following chapters will help you alleviate these fears. If you did not have intact energy you would not be here. It may currently be suppressed or running in counterproductive patterns . . . but it exists and that's what matters.

PART 2

ACCESSING YOUR GIFTS

Science now has the tools and knowledge to look at anxiety beyond its label and symptoms. Anxiety, like all of your other emotions, is a form of energy in motion. It turns out, emotions such as anxiety, anger, fear, hatred, and sadness vibrate at a lower frequency than emotions such as courage, love, and compassion. This has been measured and calibrated by great researchers such as author and American psychiatrist Dr. David R. Hawkins (*Power vs. Force*). Your gifts rest within the higher vibrations. These next few chapters are dedicated to helping you access them.

CHAPTER 4

PHASE ONE: INCREASE YOUR VIBRATION

"Your body is an absolute mirror of your mind. As you worry, your body shows it. As you love, your body shows it. As you are overwhelmed, your body shows it. As you are angry, your body shows it. Every cell of your body is being allowed or resisted by the way you feel. My physical state is a direct reflection of how I feel, instead of how I feel is a direct reflection of my physical state."

—ESTHER HICKS, INSPIRATIONAL SPEAKER AND AUTHOR

Get Ready for Your Transformation

Now that you know how anxiety works, as well as the messages it could be sending you, it is time to learn exactly how to access your gifts. The gifts are the end product of the experience of transformation. This chapter introduces a three-phase process:

1. Increase your vibration
2. Purify
3. Harmonize

Within each phase are tools and strategies that will strengthen your energy, which in turn increases your ability to diminish and transform the symptoms of anxiety. In truth, there are countless ways to get in touch with your inner self—I could never fit all of them into this book. The possibilities are endless. However, rest assured that I've included options here that are powerful and effective, especially for dealing with anxiety.

Before beginning, take a moment and reflect on a big day in your life. Perhaps you were a bit unsure whether the outcome of the event would be positive or negative—regardless, something inside told you it was significant. You might have felt nervous or had butterflies in your stomach. You know—the sort of sensations you have the night before a performance, sports event, or special occasion. Now imagine approaching these experiences without any of these sensations. No butterflies, goosebumps, or nervousness.

The event would not be the same in your memory, would it? Often the sensations leading up to the event rather than the event itself imprint on your memory bank. The imprint is not only on your conscious mind (what you are currently aware of) but also on your subconscious mind (what you may not be aware of). Research shows emotions play a large role in memory retention, meaning you are more likely to store the memory of the experience when it is connected to an emotion. Transformation works in the same way. Your transformation will be very powerful if you make it while connected to your emotions in a deep, meaningful way.

During the process of transformation, you are likely to experience physical shifts in your body. For example, as you learn the skill of breathing you may feel energy rise and fall, matching the rhythm of your breath. Or as you learn tapping or meditation, you may begin to feel a tingly sensation on your skin or even isolated tension (e.g., in your jaw). The tension could be a sign that a negative emotion is coming up to the surface to be released. Think of that tension as a *good* thing, and allow yourself to observe it without judgment. For example, instead of thinking, *Ugh, I have so much tension in my jaw,* close your eyes and experience it as if you were watching a sunrise. The more you focus on your tension as bad, the more likely it will grow. By noticing it with nonjudgment, you raise your vibration to higher states of mind, such as kindness, compassion, and love. These higher states dissipate the tension, whereas focusing on the tension will only increase negativity and fear.

While acquiring the gifts, you will go through energetic, neurological, and perceptual changes. This allows you to view what is happening inside you as well as around you in a new fashion. Since your internal systems are always changing, you really are not the same person today as you were yesterday. Your body makes millions of new cells every day—your physical body changes constantly, even if it doesn't feel like it. Your brain and neurological connections modify and adjust moment to moment, depending on not only what you are paying attention to but also the quality of your thoughts and the energy they are sourced from.

Here are some general tips to remember as you learn the techniques:

- **Start with the techniques that seem like a good match for you.** As you read over the tools, focus most on the ones that resonate with you. The others might feel like a better fit for you at some later point. However, always begin with what feels right for you.
- **Avoid trying to do everything at once.** Less is more. Read them all and choose one or two that you are willing to commit to practicing.
- **Take it easy.** Know that the process of transformation does not need to take long. Many people avoid stepping on the path of transformation because they consciously or subconsciously believe it will take a long time to get to where they want to be. This is not necessarily true. Evidence shows that when people learn how to engage their higher levels of awareness (consciousness), the process accelerates. I have seen people transform how they view their situations and thus their behavior in five weeks. The key is to take these techniques and practice. As you proceed, allow yourself time to sit back and receive what each technique has to offer.
- **Favor a nonjudgmental mindset.** If you are inclined to try to skip over these techniques and prejudge the experience as a waste of time, you may not be ready to change your patterns. Anxiety is a habitual way of being, and depending on how you have handled your symptoms in the past, you most likely have patterned your energy a certain way.
- **Stay committed.** Choose strategies that you feel most connected to and treat them like brushing your teeth. You will be using them regularly, sometimes two or three times daily. As you become able to embody a particular strategy— meaning it no longer seems like work or requires much thought or effort—then you're ready to add others to your life.
- **Your approach doesn't need to be set in stone.** At times you may find yourself alternating and trying out different

techniques. Just like the seasons change, so do your body, energy levels, and emotional, physical, and spiritual needs. This is how your body rebalances itself. When one area (energy center) is in balance, the body will naturally attempt to balance others. Therefore, keep an open mind, play around, and revisit this chapter as needed.

Phase One: Increase Your Vibration

You are an energetic being harnessed in a physical body. You are made of some of the tiniest particles known to man, such as molecules, atoms, protons, and neutrons, as well as oxygen and carbon dioxide. Your emotions are actually made up of energy too—they are a vibration of those molecules and atoms. When your vibration is strong and energetic, your body is too. When your vibration is stagnant or heavy, so is your body. Anxiety and its symptoms are your body's way of leading you to an awareness of the state of your vibration. As you read this chapter, you will learn how to recognize this force and also how to increase it in volume and strength, no matter where you are or what you are doing.

Your subconscious mind contains recordings and patterns of your life's journey in the form of energy and vibrations. Consciously, you have some understanding and association with them. It is likely to be information you have learned or witnessed during different stages of your life. According to author Patti Sparrow in *Stepping Stones*, each and every one of us has a unique signature vibration, and when lower vibrations surface, it is often the body's attempt to go back to its original signature state. Through conscious stimulation, awareness, circulation, and movement, your energy can be uplifted and therefore metamorphosed into vibration, where you can easily access, deepen, and embody your gifts. Your signature vibration is part of it.

Locating Your Gifts

Much of what you'll do in Phase 1 will help you access the space where your gifts are located. The location of your gifts has been described by many. Authors such as Dr. Wayne Dyer refer to it as "the gap," the space between thoughts you might tune into while practicing mediation. Some may experience it as the pause between words, where you would insert a comma or musical beat. The gifts are where you vibrate. You know you have landed upon them when you feel alive, focused, connected, and free. Therefore, they are highly connected to your purpose and what you love. Your gifts are in the space where creativity sparks, insight springs, and inner trust develops. Many of you have stumbled upon, stepped over, or noticed these gifts in others. They exist for you. When you become preoccupied with getting rid of or preventing the symptoms of anxiety in yourself and others, they are sacrificed.

Set Your Intentions

Intention setting grounds your energy while simultaneously activating your vibration. Once you set an intention, the laws of the universe come into play. The law of perpetual transmutation of energy states that "all persons have within them the power to change the conditions of their lives." These laws were formulated by one of the greatest scientists of all time, Sir Isaac Newton. The universe will help your intention come to pass just by you stating it. These laws have been in existence for hundreds of years and provide vital information for how to live a life of full energy and abundance. Intention setting is different from setting a goal. The following table helps outline the difference.

Goal	Intention
Mind/thinking-focused	Heart-focused
Future	Here and now
Accompanied by a plan	Accompanied by vibration
Has a target or view in mind	Free from agenda

An example of a goal would be: "I want to finish nursing school by the fall of 2016." An intention, however, would sound something like: "I choose to feel knowledgeable and empowered to make decisions about my future." Another example of a goal is "I want to learn how to meditate" and an intention might be "I feel drawn to people and resources that teach meditation." Another goal might be to "make more money." An intention might be "I choose to notice how generous and abundant my own energy is."

Think of your intention as your initial energy deposit. You will deposit some energy as if it were money in a bank. You will watch it grow and then be able to utilize it. Taking the time to foster what you already have—a supply of perfect energy—makes what you desire come more easily and naturally. For example, you may want to be more peaceful, loving, and patient. As you part ways with the symptoms of anxiety and put forth your intentions, you will naturally shift in this way.

Exercise: What Is Your Intention?

Take a moment and ask yourself, what is your intention? To feel better, more connected, alive, or peaceful? Perhaps you want to improve how you communicate, have more loving relationships, or be able to let go of the past. Go ahead and dream about what you want. Close your eyes, take a long inhale and exhale, and just imagine what it would feel like if it came true. If you can't even imagine what you might want, make up something, and then imagine what it would feel like to realize that desire.

The words you use to state your intention are important as well. You want to state it as if it already *is*, rather than as something you want or that *will be* at some point. The following table shows you how to set an intention using words and relevant imagery.

Instead of Saying . . .	Say . . .	Think of This Image	Imagine This Sound
I want peace	I choose peace	Rainbow	Running water
I should let go	I choose to let go	Leaves falling	Wind blowing
I am going to make money	I have worth	Mountaintops	Sound of thunder
I desire clarity	I create clarity	Sunrise	Bell

As always, do what works for you. There is no right or wrong image to think about. One person may connect clarity to an image of wipers clearing a windshield, while another may make the connection through the sound of a chime or the ocean lapping against the shoreline. Scenes in nature that match the tone and feelings of the intention seem to work well.

Create an Intention Related to Anxiety

Once you're comfortable with the process of setting an intention, you can create one that's relevant to your symptoms of anxiety. If you want an anxiety-free life, your intention might be something like "I am choosing confidence, trust, and resiliency." You might think of a sturdy rock in the middle of a roaring river. Allow yourself a moment to hear the rumble and feel the steadiness. In that moment, you are the rock. You may also choose to set an intention like "I choose to accept the gifts already inside me."

Intentions in Action

Many people find that setting intentions helps them ground themselves when they feel overwhelmed by life. For example, Rhonda was the mother of two young children. For years she struggled with depression and anxiety. In her marriage, she felt alone and isolated because her husband often worked long hours, leaving her little time for herself. In the years prior she had taken medication off and on to help manage her symptoms. Once again, she felt she needed help but really did not want to go the same route she did before. Instead, she wanted to find more mindful ways to help herself through. She began this process by developing her intentions. She indicated that she wanted to feel better, have more energy, and be less overwhelmed with her busy, restricted lifestyle. Symptoms of both depression and anxiety can feel heavy in the body, and she wanted to feel lighter in both body and spirit. Depression zapped her energy while anxiety made her feel stuck and unhappy. Her intentions addressed those issues.

Rhonda chose these intentions:

- I choose to feel energy.
- I choose freedom from stress.
- I choose feeling lighter.

At first, stating her intentions in this way felt unfamiliar and uncomfortable to her. However, as she closed her eyes and repeated the intention, utilizing the approach of imagining (seeing and hearing) her intention, she began to feel more capable and competent. She then expanded her visualization by imagining her judgments of herself running like water down her spine and off her body.

Get in Touch with Your Emotional Frequency

The tools you are about to learn—grounding, breathing, lighting up your hands, energy techniques, tapping, and meditation—elevate your emotional frequency. By utilizing them, you stimulate and expand the movement of energy in your body. Since emotions are energy in motion, practices such as these convert lower vibrational states, such as worry, into hope or assurance. States of hope and appreciation resonate more with your heart. The heart not only magnifies what you project into the world, but also, with awareness, helps you purify thoughts, emotions, and beliefs that no longer serve you (more on this later in the chapter).

Many of us have been conditioned to see our emotions as inherently good or bad. It's time to think about them in an entirely different way now. Your emotions are not bad or good— what's important is how and if they are moving. Picture yourself in a crowd of people at an amazing concert. If the crowd is packed to the point where you can't move or see the stage, you may feel frustrated. But if the crowd is moving, dancing, and singing you may also feel energized and uplifted. To truly free yourself from the symptoms of anxiety, you will need to put your attention on what liberates you rather than what binds you. Instead of seeing the uncomfortably packed room, see the opportunity to experience the music with all the other fans.

Grounding Exercises

Feeling imbalanced, shaky, and a tad ambivalent about life? Try incorporating grounding exercises into your day. The word *ground* makes you think of the earth and soil—raw material that all plants and trees grow from. Likewise, grounding your energy is a way to secure your resiliency and strength in the here and now.

Grounding yourself also:

1. Increases circulation while providing balance and stability
2. Retrains your energy to uplift rather than deplete you

The second point is especially important because anxiety and its symptoms create a habitual response of giving away energy. The following grounding exercises will retrain the parts of your body that are conditioned to drop or send energy away to instead cultivate it. One of these areas is your solar plexus (found two inches above your navel). When energy is depleted in this area, you may feel powerless or helpless. This is why so many people feel upset in their stomach when they are anxious or eat as a way to manage the discomfort of missing energy. When you instead increase energy in this area, you are able to see the choices in your life, make clear decisions, and hear and trust your inner voice.

Following are three ways to ground your energy.

Be Sure to Ground Yourself Before Breathing

You may have been taught to breathe the moment you begin to feel worried or anxious. Breathing is important; however, the effectiveness of your breathing will be far more powerful if you ground yourself first. Otherwise, you risk breathing ineffectively (through upper-chest breathing), which actually increases the symptoms of anxiety.

Learning to ground your energy before breathing not only anchors you in your body but also stabilizes your joints. For example, before initiating your breathing, it is important to put two feet on the floor and sit up tall. This creates space for your internal organs and for both oxygen and carbon dioxide to circulate. Without grounding first, you may compress your organs by leaning forward or slouching and therefore prevent the expulsion of carbon dioxide. This can leave you feeling uneasy, dizzy, anxious, and depressed.

Tap Into Your Larger Muscle Groups

Your quadriceps (thighs) and biceps are two examples of large muscle groups. Many people are drawn toward exercises that use these muscles, such as squats, running, weightlifting, biking, and hiking. You may even hear them reference such activity as therapy or their form of Prozac. When you activate your intention to ground your energy while engaging in large-muscle movements, you are calling on the energy of the earth to support you. Remember, everything is energy and energy extends far beyond what you can see.

To understand how larger muscles can help you ground yourself, squeeze your fist really tight and release. After feeling the contraction of your fist, you can really appreciate the expansion you feel when you release it. That's the sensation you want to capture in your larger muscle groups. You can ground your energy using large muscle groups by walking uphill or doing a pushup on the floor. Think of yourself as anchoring your presence on this earth.

Mula Bandha

Mula bandha is often referenced in yoga as a way to teach people how to keep their bodies safe while moving. It is also the term used to refer to the muscles utilized in your genital area (pelvic region). Mula bandha is taught as a technique for circulating lower-vibrating energy that can become locked up in the pelvic area, such as feelings of grief and shame. The easiest is to squeeze the muscles in your genital area (the ones you squeeze and hold when you have to go to the bathroom). This is commonly referred to as Kegels. By squeezing and releasing these muscles, you can:

- Interrupt negative thoughts
- Strengthen your bladder muscles
- Lift and ground your energy

Take a moment and (without squeezing these muscles) think of something negative or something that bothers you—say, when you see someone litter or drive recklessly. It can even just be a negative word like *hate*. Now, squeeze your mula bandha really tight until you experience tension in your face. Then decrease the squeeze just enough so that your jaw releases. You will know this because your back teeth will separate. Maintain this slight squeeze (about 30 percent of a full squeeze) with your jaw released and again bring this same negativity into your mind and notice how it is difficult to capture. It is like a piece of tape that will not stick.

According to David Life, founder of Jivamukti Yoga, "Mula bandha is said to cut through *brahma granthi*, the energetic knot of our resistance to change." It is an exercise that has been around for thousands of years and it contributes to the practice of transformation. Uplifting energy means to uproot resistance without engaging in an internal power struggle. Part of you may want change, while the other part holds on to things staying the same. Instead of struggling with your mind, incorporate mula bandha exercises into your daily life (e.g., while you sit at your desk or drive a car). Picture a baseball game where a player announces to his teammates, *I've got this one* and catches the ball.

Mula bandha exercises are your way of saying to your mind, *Let go, my body is handling this.*

Visualization: Grounding Yourself

We'll talk more in depth about visualizations later in this chapter. For now, consider trying this visualization:

Sit up tall and close your eyes. Imagine the sun way above your head shining its rays down on your body. Feel the warmth of the sun penetrate the crown of your head and down into your body. Allow it to spread throughout your face, neck, down your arms, torso, heart, hips, thighs, and way down into the soles of your feet. Relax your entire body and feel the sensation on the bottom of your toes, inner arches of your feet, and heels.

Now imagine roots growing from your feet into the earth. These roots both anchor and nourish your entire being. Allow your roots to spread far beyond where your eyes can see and deep into the earth. As you breathe, imagine receiving stability, strength, and nourishment.

Gift Tag

Meditation: Walking Barefoot

Walking barefoot can help you ground yourself by really noticing and receiving what the earth is offering you. Take off your shoes and practice walking slowly and mindfully outside in the grass, dirt, or sand. Notice how you become more sensitive to the earth and how it feeds you. Pay attention to the way your feet hit the ground, and how the weight is distributed between the ball of your foot, heels, and toes. Notice the texture and temperature of the ground. Do this for two or three minutes while taking deep breaths.

Breathing

Your breath lets you know whether you are choosing to brace or embrace the moments of your day:

- The energy of brace pulls you out of your body, away from your breath. It does this most likely out of habit as a way to get you through the day. Bracing feels like your mind and body have separated; they are no longer one. For example, imagine listening to someone who is highly intellectual but boring. She may speak with very little feeling, use limited voice inflection, or speak in terminology you cannot understand. You may find yourself working hard to pay attention. Eventually, you may begin to experience tension and, as a result, become distracted. You may even think, *How much longer do I have to sit through this?* or *How can I get out of this situation?* This is what it feels like to brace yourself. It is the way you push yourself through uncomfortable feelings by thinking.
- To embrace means you are opening up your breath, and allowing the energy of your spirit to flow through your body. Embracing is similar to how you might pull aside the curtains and open the window as a way to take in the new day.

You'll find your gifts within the space where you embrace your energy. To fully sense this space, first clear the energy of bracing. After taking a deep inhale and exhale, ask yourself to notice how you may be carrying the energy of brace. For example, do you find yourself preparing for the experience of other people's emotions? Or perhaps you brace yourself for your own emotions. If this resonates with you, give yourself permission to close your eyes, take a long inhale (through your nose), and exhale (through your nose) while choosing to clear the energy of brace.

Why Technique Is Important

Breathing is one of the quickest ways to move energy that no longer serves you. *How* you breathe, however, makes a difference. Shallow upper-chest breathing can actually exasperate symptoms of anxiety by increasing your blood pressure, heart rate, thoughts, and rushing behavior. Taking time to slow down your breathing will be of great service to you in so many areas of your life. Instead of shallow, upper-chest breathing, you want to access the lower lobes of your lungs, where many calming nerves are located. To do so, you will practice inhaling and exhaling, taking air in and letting it out at equal lengths or with the exhale one count longer. Breathing through your nose increases calming sensations. This may not be something you are accustomed to, so take some time to get used to the feeling.

Mary and Rick NurrieStearns state in their book *Yoga for Anxiety* that consciously slowing down your breathing triggers the relaxation response, which is "medicine" for anxiety. They recommend becoming a witness of your breath at first: simply notice it, rather than attempting to deepen or manipulate it. Then, silently repeat the words *breath coming in and breath going out* as you engage in this process.

Guidelines for Breathing

- Begin by softening your gaze: Instead of looking up or straight ahead, set your gaze a few feet in front of you on the floor. Place your feet flat on the floor for grounding. Sit upright, sliding your head back so your chin is parallel to the floor. Roll your shoulders around a few times to help your body settle in. Relax your hands on your lap or by your sides. Lean back so your diaphragm has room to rise and fall.
- On inhale, your belly inflates like a balloon. You will feel the breath not only push your belly out but also inflate the sides

of your waist. It may help you to put your hand on your lower abdomen (below the navel) so you can direct your breath and attention to your lower belly. Inhale, counting one, two, three.

- On exhale, your belly deflates and moves toward your spine. You will feel like you are squeezing your lower abdomen into a pair of tight pants. Your navel will press in and slightly up. You may either exhale at equal lengths, counting one, two, three, or hold on the count of four.

Other Breathing Techniques

The following two breathing methods might also be useful as you become more comfortable with monitoring your breathing.

Gather, Store, Distribute

This breath technique was taken from author and yoga instructor Sarah Powers. She describes the inhale as gathering the energy in the body. To facilitate this process, contract mula bandha (discussed earlier in this chapter)—slightly squeeze the muscles that control your flow of urine. Imagine yourself gathering rose petals or fresh fruit in a basket—this will help you stimulate sensations connected to peace and gratitude. The next step is to store this energy in your lower belly and pelvic area. Think of storing as filling your pelvis with energy that is vibrant, colorful, and energizing.

The final step is to release, and imagine and allow the energy of these higher frequencies to distribute itself throughout your body.

Left-Nostril Breathing

This technique has been around for thousands of years and has been proven to alleviate symptoms of stress and anxiety. Close off your right nostril with your thumb and inhale and exhale through your left nostril (with your mouth closed) five or six times, slowly and consciously (closing your eyes can help). Count to three with your inhale and exhale. Why the left nostril? It helps you stimulate the right hemisphere of your brain (consciousness) while activating the part of your nervous system that promotes calming and relaxation (your parasympathetic nervous system). It turns out your nostrils do not breathe evenly, meaning there are certain times during the day when you are naturally breathing through your right nostril more. If you feel jittery, impulsive, or find yourself rushing through tasks, consider blocking your right nostril and breathing exclusively through the left for three to five breaths. This is a simple way to restore inner balance.

Gift Tag

Exercise: Breath Sounds

Take a moment and listen to the sounds around you. Notice which sounds resemble your inhale, as well as the ones that mimic your exhale. You might think of the wind blowing, chimes, crickets, the sound of a train, the hum of your refrigerator, running water . . . ask yourself, *How do they remind me of my breath?* As you breathe in and out of your nose, listen to the sounds generated in the back of your throat. Also, remember that not all living things make a sound—for example, consider too the silence of the grass growing. Tune in to this silence and pay attention to how this makes you feel.

Stretching Your Energy

Anxiety is known not only for its inflexible, rigid thinking, but also for those tight, uncomfortable knots you may find in your back, neck, or stomach. These knots may bring about additional symptoms, such as headaches and tightness. The energy is so compact and tight it can feel as if you could snap it. Just like you can increase flexibility in your body through physical stretches, you can also engage in exercises that spread your energy. These include: light up your hands, exercise, stretching, energy techniques, tapping, and meditation.

Stretching your energy opens up your mind, body, and soul. Not only does it increase the volume of energy but also the strength and clarity of information you receive. When your body is tight, your energy is like a protective cocoon around you. The cocoon technique may help you get through a traumatic situation; however, if the cocoon remains in place over a long period of time, it may prevent you from receiving the love around you—including from people, nature, and experiences, as well as from yourself. As a result, you will probably experience less satisfaction with your relationships, job, and overall life. You may have everything you need, but still long for something more. Following are ways to stretch and strengthen your energy.

Heal with Your Hands

Discovering the power of your own hands is one of the quickest and easiest ways to lift your vibration. Your hands are electromagnetic—similar to magnets, they can attract and move energy. Your hands were perfectly designed for self-healing. Studies have shown that therapeutic touch (such as acupressure) as well as nontouch modalities (such as Reiki) alleviate and clear away symptoms of anxiety while increasing balance and harmony.

Starting Out

This technique may be foreign to you at first, but keep an open mind.

1. To begin, rub your hands together vigorously for thirty seconds with your fingers pressed together.
2. Move your hands several inches apart and you are likely to feel the energy between them. The stronger the feel, the more movement there is (i.e., molecules in motion). Try this repeatedly and notice how your hands want to magnetically move closer together while at the same time grow apart.
3. Rub your hands together and then raise them to the sides of your head, by your ears, and feel the energy radiating around you as if you were blowing up a bubble outside of your body. Hold them there with the palms facing in. Keep your fingers sealed together when you do this. Take a deep breath and if you like, circle your hands clockwise. Feel how big and radiant you are.

Once you can feel the energy in your hands, picture it as a water spring that never runs dry. It will always replenish itself. It is your open heart and nonjudgmental attitude that maintains the flow. The moment you think to yourself, *I can't feel anything*, notice how easily panic or disbelief sets in. Your thoughts suppress the flow. Relax, close your eyes, unhinge your jaw, and you will notice how this influences your breath and therefore your flow of energy.

Hovering over Your Chakras

If it feels right for you, practice the following technique daily to help positive energy flow. It's similar to Reiki, an energy-healing practice that uses the hands. Rub your hands together (as fast as if you were trying to get two sticks to light a spark) and then place your hands (fingers together) in front of your energy centers. These are also known as chakras:

1. Heart
2. Throat
3. Forehead
4. Above and below your navel
5. Pelvic area
6. A few inches above your head

Hover over each area as you allow the movement to push your hand away and draw it forward. If your energy feels weak in a particular area, spend a minute or so circling above it while you take deep breaths until it feels stronger.

By moving your hands in a clockwise position (again, with fingers sealed) a few inches above these energy centers, either while you lie down or sit up tall, you increase the flow of your energy. You are likely to find it only takes a few minutes with your eyes closed for you to feel a sense of calm. Do this daily and you will retrain your energy to run smoothly and efficiently.

Energy-Healing Techniques

Science's law of energy states that energy cannot be created or destroyed, but it can be transformed from one form to another, or transferred from one object to another. "Energy healing" refers to techniques that move energy in an effort to correct imbalances that can show up in the form of physical, emotional, or mental distress. Energy healing can be done on yourself or on others. Once you truly grasp and experience the power of working with energy, you can even utilize it as a way to strengthen your resiliency or break up the negative energy in a room.

Before You Begin

Donna Eden, the pioneer of energy medicine, recommends exercises that increase blood flow between the right and left hemisphere of your brain and also support the flow of energy in the organs, glands, muscles, tissues, etc. Marching in place and calming triple warmer (see the following sections) are two techniques Donna suggests. Anxiety, when sustained over time, immobilizes your energy, so you need to work at getting it moving again. To encourage blood flow between hemispheres, try:

1. Marching in place
2. Slapping a knee with the opposite hand

Also, tapping acupressure points with two fingers while inhaling and exhaling through the mouth can help strengthen your energy so that you are able to recognize and experience shifts in the body more easily. Your hands—particularly your fingertips (where there are many nerve endings)—can promote relaxation through pressing and massaging. Simply by pinching the sides of the fingertips or massaging each finger while giving each a gentle tug calms your nervous system and deepens your ability to breathe (particularly to exhale).

Another acupressure point specific to alleviating anxiety is on your wrist. To find this point, place your index, middle, and ring fingers together, and lay them at the crease of your wrist. You'll find the acupressure point between the two tendons in the middle of your wrist, where your index finger crosses these tendons. Apply steady pressure there with your finger.

Balance Your Triple Warmer

Following are some ways to calm down what is referred to as triple warmer (TW). The TW is an energy meridian that governs your fight, flight, or freeze response. Consider your meridians to be your invisible energy transportation centers. You cannot see them, but they can be measured and experienced. Michelle Earnest, a practitioner of energy medicine, states, "When the TW is out of balance, it pulls energy from the spleen meridian to keep itself in overdrive. This makes the spleen weak and unable to help you stay emotionally well and stable." Therefore, techniques that help TW regain balance are essential. See the following exercises.

Calm Down TW Technique #1

Place the fingertips of both hands in the middle of your forehead, press down, then gently drag and trace your fingers across to above your ears, circle around the back of your ears, to the bottom of your earlobes, and then travel your fingers down your neck to the middle of your heart. Do this three to four times while inhaling and exhaling through your mouth. The calm you feel means your energy is flowing.

Calm Down TW Technique #2

K27 is the twenty-seventh acupressure point on the kidney meridian. In Chinese medicine, when someone is feeling agitated or angry, it is common to look to relieving these symptoms by creating energy flow in this meridian. You may also tap this area repeatedly with two fingers while inhaling and exhaling. Then take your fingers and tap your breastbone (above your sternum) in the middle of your chest. For video instruction, go to *www.youtube .com/watch?v=jeQsNloODmY.*

Tapping (EFT)

Emotional freedom technique, also known as tapping, is a safe technique that blends psychology with Chinese acupressure. It is based on the philosophy that stagnant, negative emotions can be stored in the energy of the body. By tapping on certain points on the face and body, that old energy will move. As a result, many people report relief from symptoms such as pain, anxiety, and stress. In addition, since your body is connected to your subconscious mind, you also gain an awareness of the thoughts and beliefs that are looking to be released. Tapping is great for individuals who want to work with their thoughts, name them, and claim them.

Please note there are a variety of tapping techniques. Some involve focusing on your breathing, while other techniques (such as EFT) allow you to speak your thoughts out loud.

The following tapping exercise is taken from *The Tapping Solution*, by Nick Ortner. He suggests that you begin with a setup statement such as: *Even though_____, I deeply and completely love myself.* So, for example, you may say, *Even though I feel sad, angry, or frustrated, I deeply and completely love myself.* Continue to speak out loud what you are feeling either emotionally or physically while tapping. To do the tapping part of the exercise, use one hand to tap with your index and middle fingers at least seven times before moving on to the next location. Tap each of these eight points:

1. The inner corner of your eyebrow
2. The side of your eye (near your temple)
3. Under your eye on your cheekbone
4. Under your nose (on the space above your top lip)
5. The middle of your chin
6. Your collarbone
7. Under your arm
8. The top of your head

You do this for several rounds until you feel your energy start to move. You will know it has moved when you feel the emotion or pain has toned down a notch or two. Tapping will never hurt you and can be done anywhere at any time. The more often you practice, the better the results.

Meditating

Meditation is a way to quiet your mind, focus your attention, and help you to develop the skill of awareness in both your mind and body. Its ability to increase your alpha brain wave activity (which indicates a state of relaxation) is powerfully transformative, helping you to release subconscious beliefs and fear while increasing vibration. It is known for its positive impact on performance, memory, communication skills, health, and overall quality of life. With practice, it can create new neurological patterns that support good energy flow.

In the book *The Mindful Way through Depression*, by Mark Williams, John Teasdale, Zindel Segal, and Jon Kabat-Zinn, meditation is described as mindfully attending to your feelings. Instead of avoiding them, you approach them through a natural curiosity and attention. The authors state, "instead of triggering fervent efforts to reject the 'unacceptable' emotions that pass through us, we meet them with a sense of acceptance . . . The openhearted approach attitude of mindfulness provides an antidote to the instinctive avoidance that can fuel rumination." Rumination is a symptom of both anxiety and depression. Rumination is the constant circulation and festering of your thoughts. Thoughts are sticky, similar to how a piece of lint sticks easily to tape. Rumination runs the thoughts through your mind habitually, without awareness. For example, if you were working and started to feel irritated and frustrated, you may hear yourself complaining about how much you hate your job or saying that you can't wait until the day ends. Or you may unconsciously numb your thoughts by attempting to stop them through self-distraction. This may occur through wandering via texting, checking e-mails, eating, or procrastination.

Meditation naturally creates space between your thoughts in a way that honors your feelings. This helps you develop a new relationship between old thoughts and unresolved feelings. Rather than pushing away discomfort, antsy feelings, or fidgety behaviors, through the process of meditation you can learn to recognize the possible shifts that are taking place in your body. Instead of immediately reacting to them, you learn to experience your feelings. The ocean tide is one metaphor for meditation. The tide moves effortlessly toward and away from the shoreline. Old stagnant energy is moving out, while new, higher-vibrational energy moves in.

How to Meditate

Meditation can be practiced in a couple of minutes, one hour, or more. It can be done while sitting, walking, drinking a cup of tea, or performing a routine task such as sweeping or washing the dishes. With mindfulness, it is possible for you to go in and out of meditative states throughout the day.

Small actions, such as placing your feet on the floor, momentarily closing your eyes, taking a deep inhale and long exhale, and pausing to feel the warm sun or gentle rain on your face are simple ways to tell your mind and body that you are choosing to soak up the moment. The present moment is where your gifts are located. Anxiety cannot live in the present moment; it only resides in the future or lingers around the past. By choosing to mindfully engage the moment, you inevitably enter the space where your gifts reside.

A Simple Meditation

1. Prepare your space: If you are in your home, choose a comfortable chair to sit in, or find a place to sit outside. If your space has bright lighting, you may want to turn it down. Close yourself off from any harsh distractions, such as loud noises coming from a window. You may benefit from downloading soothing meditative sounds (ocean, birds, flute) onto your iPod or smartphone so that you are able to use earphones.

2. Prepare your body: Sit down and place your feet on the floor. As you sit up tall, you give your internal organs the space needed to breathe. Close your eyes or soften your gaze a few feet in front of you on the floor.

3. Tune in: This process is similar to tuning in to a particular radio station, except you tune in to your vibration. Allow your awareness to rest inside and notice how your breath begins to expand. Choose to watch this while noticing (without judgment) the tingling sensations that arise. If thoughts arise, that is normal. You are human and it is not possible to shut them out completely. The most important part is to accept this as true and to avoid placing a value on your meditation. So you get distracted—it is not a big deal, so be mindful of how you respond to that. Notice if you say to yourself, *This isn't working* or *I better stop; my kids need me.* Instead, be grateful for that one minute of quieting your mind; it is worth far more than you could ever imagine. Treat it like it is a piece of gold. Before you know it, you will be able to quiet your mind no matter what you are doing—washing the dishes, folding laundry, or walking to the mailbox.

Eventually, you will develop a bit of a ritual. For example, you may use the same chair, or meditate around the same time each day. The early morning before your day is in full swing or right before you go to bed works best for many people.

Meditation Tips and Tricks

- Meditation is not sleep. You are awake and aware of what is happening both inside and outside of you.
- Instead of trying to avoid your thoughts and urges you are noticing them without judgment. For example, if you hear your phone beep, give yourself permission to take a deep breath and notice the feeling and triggered thoughts that accompany that moment. Then return to your meditation. The more you practice the easier it will be.
- Allow each practice to be unique. Some days your meditations will be longer and deeper than others.
- Be open to finding attachments. Meditation is a clearing of the mind: this includes what is real, unreal, what is truth, and what are lies. Meditation gives you permission to circulate all of it freely. In return, you receive valuable information about your attachments (what you may be clinging to) as well as how your body sets you free. Attachments often come up as thoughts about what is bothering you, weighing on your mind, or charging your emotions. Charged emotions are ones that you revisit regularly through storytelling and inner dialogue. If you find your negative thoughts are increasing, picture something in your mind that you appreciate, perhaps the smile of a loved one or the smell of lilacs.

Gift Tag

Skill: Guided Supports

You may find that you respond better to guided meditations. Typically, a teacher of meditation talks you through the practice, giving you things to visualize and experience along the way. (Guided meditations can be purchased on iTunes or on a CD—look for Jon Kabat-Zinn's meditations.) You can also visualize on your own, of course. You may have an image of a place that you have been or not been that warms your heart—or try something as simple as a meadow, willow tree, stream of water, or mountaintops.

What If I Don't Feel Anything?

If you are like most people new to exploring energy, at first you may not feel anything. Stay calm; you are not broken. At first, you just may be overthinking it. Similar to when your car battery stops working, sometimes your energy system needs to be charged up.

Aerobic exercises (particularly ones that have you cross your midline) such as climbing, swimming, dancing, yoga, tai chi, and many more can help you jump-start your energy. It is important to change up your routine now and then so all your muscles have a chance to work and your energy is forced to move in different directions.

If you don't feel like working out, then consider stretching or doing some gentle yoga. Many times, people look at stretching as something you have to do or should do. Stretching not only lengthens and protects your tissue and muscles, but it also builds flexibility in the mind. It is a simple way to feel energy and can be done just about anywhere. At work in your chair you might stretch your arms overhead, gently twist side to side, lift up your chin and let your head fall back to stretch your neck, and more. To release tension in your jaw, you can even open your mouth wide, and stretch out your tongue. You might be surprised to see how much relief you receive from that simple exercise.

Stretching connects you to your breath and softens your gaze, making you less susceptible to picking up the stress in your environment. It feels good and increases the amount of sensation you feel in your body. Here's a quick list of things you can do to jump-start your connection to your energy:

1. Breathing exercises
2. Engage in exercises that cross the midline (e.g., right arm goes to the left side of the body)
3. Climbing (engaging large muscles)
4. Gardening (connecting to earth)
5. Swimming (breast stroke, cross kicks)
6. Stretching (e.g., place your arms out in front of you, cross them like an X, and hold your shoulders to stretch your shoulders and back)

If you're feeling stuck, sometimes practicing these simple moves can bring you a little closer to accessing your energy.

Still Thinking More Than Feeling?

Have you ever heard the phrase "What you resist persists"? The same is true with your thoughts. If you attempt to resist, push away, or stop yourself from accepting your thoughts, they will most likely return—not only magnified but multiplied. Deepak Chopra's law of least effort states that "nature's intelligence functions with effortless ease . . . with carefreeness, harmony, and love."

Chopra also states, "Least effort is expended when your actions are motivated by love." Stopping, pushing away, or telling yourself that the experiences in your life are just not worth anything are nonloving responses. How you treat yourself is highly connected to your ability to access your gifts. Love yourself and you'll find your gifts closer than you thought.

CHAPTER 5

PHASE TWO: PURIFY

"It's pleasing to discover that it isn't necessary to drive oneself forward; instead, one can simply allow oneself to move forward as blocks are removed. Thus, one becomes attracted by the future rather than propelled by the past."

—DR. DAVID R. HAWKINS, *ALONG THE PATH TO ENLIGHTENMENT*

What Is Purifying?

Now that you have increased your connections to the sensations in your body, and provided the space for inner energy movement, it is time to purify your emotions. Purifying your emotions helps you take things less personally—instead you feel open, lighter, compassionate, and forgiving. This section teaches you four ways to do this:

1. Making the choice
2. Giving permission
3. Diving into your emotions
4. Visualization and sound

Purifying emotions is like deleting old programs from your computer. These programs are likely to slow it down or in some cases cause it to crash. You may also think of the process as a filter. Impurities and toxins are removed so that your system is able to metabolize and digest what you put in it more easily. Anxiety and its symptoms are representations of old programs that at one point ran clearly, but now have become jammed into your system, clogging the connections between your heart, mind, and body. By clearing away the old systems, you make way for new ones (perceptions and experiences). Keep in mind, your computer has to be plugged in to be able to filter out what is not working. Increasing your vibrational frequency first (as discussed in Phase 1) automatically "plugs" you into this phase.

Although the three phases are laid out as separate steps, with practice they will flow together. When you get to that point with practice, you'll find what you need much quicker. However, during the purification process there are two important things for you to know:

1. You have to choose to purify.
2. It is important to give your body permission to purify.

Anxiety takes hold of your mind. You can tell yourself and others a million times, *I no longer want the symptoms*—however, until you give your body permission (through your conscious and subconscious mind), you may find yourself feeling like you're swimming upstream. Until you've made a choice and given yourself permission, you might feel that freeing yourself from the symptoms takes a tremendous amount of effort.

Because you lifted your vibration first, you are more likely to view your world with more awareness. This opens you up to insight and wisdom. Therefore, anything that comes your way becomes a significant part of your gift journey. When you're open to insight, you might find it arrives at a later point in the day, well after you've meditated, tapped, or breathed deeply. For example, Brenda had a daily ritual of uplifting her emotions. In the morning while drinking her coffee she would sit in her favorite chair. She would close her eyes and imagine herself being wrapped in a beautiful light coming down from the heavens. This increased the sensations she felt on her skin and she would imagine her energy rippling from her body. As she observed the sensations that moved around different parts of her body, she would silently state what she was grateful for.

One day when she was driving to work—nearly two hours after her ritual but still feeling the earlier vibrations from the morning—she looked over at the car in the next lane. It was a truck with a man and a young boy in it. She noticed immediately that the boy was standing up and had no seatbelt on. She felt tension in her jaw as she held back, wanting to shout something to the man. The man looked over at her and for a moment she saw a flash of her uncle. The man not only looked similar but his actions reminded her of something her uncle would do. As he sped away, she felt the feelings of fear and uncertainty surface. Initially, they were for the boy; however, she realized the fear and uncertainty had been buried inside her. In that moment, she gave thanks and made the choice to purify them. She gave her body permission by allowing this locked-up energy to run off her shoulders, spine, and hips. Still tuned in to what energy felt like earlier that morning, the decision and process came easily. Although the car was gone by the time she thought to report it, because she took it as an opportunity to release the block it increased the likelihood that the next time she sees something potentially dangerous she will calmly report it. When you are able to take action calmly, this means you do not take the story or incident with you and it does not impact the quality of your day. Releasing blocks gives you the courage to do what feels right.

Gift Tag

Exercise: Spinal Twist

Spinal twists help your body process, purify, and digest the emotions in your body. Consider how all day long, emotions such as anxiety are surfacing as a way to catch your attention. Take a moment and sit up tall with your feet on the ground. Relax your shoulders and loosen your jaw. While relaxing your neck (keep looking straight ahead, rather than twisting your neck), place your left hand on your right thigh and gently twist your body to one side as you exhale. Inhale back to center and then place your right hand on your left thigh, and again while looking straight ahead, twist to the other side as you exhale. Inhale back to center. Notice how your energy feels fuller.

Diving In

The famous psychiatrist Carl Jung stated, "The 'other' in us always seems alien and unacceptable; but if we let ourselves be aggrieved the feeling sinks in, and we are richer for this little bit of self-knowledge." Like a good story, your emotions have a beginning, middle, and end. Experiencing and completing a feeling can take about ninety seconds. However, when they are pushed back, buried, or disregarded it may take days, months, or for some, a lifetime to let that emotion come to fruition. Diving into your emotions takes a bit of courage but is well worth the plunge. What happens when you experience your emotions is that they become purified. Similar to the process of filtering toxic impurities out of water, you are filtering lower-vibrational frequencies that are experienced as anxiety. By choosing to dive in, you are electing to purify the thoughts, feelings, and memories that divert you from your gifts. This increases the opportunities for new thoughts, feelings, ideas, and perceptions. As you dive in, you will come across different sensations. If you remain neutral and observant (rather than reactive), these sensations and physical reactions will be temporary. Some of these include:

- Shaking—an inner rattle that can feel like nervousness; it may come across as trouble sitting still or staying in one place
- Butterflies or fluttering in your stomach
- Sighing
- Yawning
- Temporary nervousness or tension
- Tingly sensations all over your body
- Teary eyes
- A sudden deep breath, as if you were coming up for air
- A feeling of surrender

You know that you have plunged into an emotion when you feel more open and detached from what you were previously attached to. For example, Brenda allowed herself to dive into uncertainty when she no longer carried the fear and disappointment that she originally felt. She was able to let go of the event, yet hold on to the wisdom she gained.

One of the best places to practice this is in the shower. The shower for many is a place where you can speak to yourself privately. It is your time to set an intention, get centered, dive in, stand naked, and state your truth. You can activate this process by stating to yourself out loud, *I notice these feelings of uncertainty and I choose to feel them.* Close your eyes as you feel the water on your skin. The following steps lead you through:

1. First you can uplift your vibration by scrubbing the shampoo into your wet hair. Press the pads of your fingers and nails into your scalp and give yourself a good scrubbing.
2. Notice how your scalp sends tingly sensations down your neck and face (vibration).
3. Next, dive in—rinse out (flush) the soap by standing still and allowing the water to roll down your head and off your body (purification). As you do, anchor and press down into the four corners of each foot. Notice the rising and falling of your breath. Also notice the parts of you that feel dull or empty. You know you have completed the emotion when you feel whole. Like a puzzle, each part of you is touching the other; in this case your mind, body, and spirit are connected.

The more you practice, the greater your ability becomes to know when something feels complete. Some emotions may be cleared through one long conscious inhale and exhale, while others may take longer. Clearing your emotions is a meditation, a way to focus your attention while giving your body and higher self permission to release anything that no longer serves you and your relationship to your gifts.

If you still feel you need support with this process, or the thought of experiencing your emotions provokes extreme fear, you will be better off practicing under the supervision of a licensed therapist or other qualified professional who has the training and certifications to support people through anxiety.

Visualizing

Through imagining scenes or images in your mind, certain emotions can be brought to the forefront and purified. For example, by picturing something in your mind you can activate the vibration of love. Many people who experience symptoms of anxiety report that they always picture the worst-case scenario. For example, they feel that they will fail, get in trouble, or disappoint others. Reactions such as these are often linked to buried emotions and misinterpretations. This section will show you how to purify emotions such as guilt and shame as well as your attachments through visual imagery.

Anxiety is a contagious emotion. Therefore, how you visually scan your environment will be important. Without awareness, you can absorb symptoms from others through your eyes. For example, you may visually pick up symptoms through reading other people's body language and facial expressions. Visualization plays a significant role in memory. You may not recall certain details of an event, but specific images or visual triggers in your environment may spark symptoms.

Individuals who have specific fears or who have been diagnosed with an anxiety disorder may need the services of a licensed psychologist to help them overcome them. Often, the process will include looking at pictures of possible triggers to help the individual work through symptoms such as increased heart rate, sweating, and nervousness.

If you have lived with the symptoms of anxiety for a long time, once again, it will be important for you to find ways to incorporate Phase 1 tools into your daily life. Once you do, if visualization appeals to you, or in general you tend to be a more visual person, this can be a creative way to purify your emotions. The following example gives you an idea of how it works.

Tom remembered that when he was a child, his father taught him that you have to work hard to be successful in life. As a result, he always worked hard. In school if he received anything less than an A, he would blame himself for not doing enough. At work, he was known to extend his hours into the night and be the first one to arrive in the morning. This lifestyle eventually took its toll, inhibiting his ability to take in and enjoy the moment. Instead he would control it through phone calls, appointments, schedules, lists, and expectations.

Once Tom learned the value of increasing his vibrations, he was more open to the idea of purifying his emotions. The increase gave him an awareness that his father taught him a great deal about work ethic and responsibility. What he did not learn from his childhood was how to let go. Rather than attempting to understand letting go intellectually, he decided to utilize visualizations. From his higher vibrational state, he would casually scan his environment for images of letting go. What he discovered was the teachings had been around him all along. For example, one day he found himself behind a garbage truck. He watched it lift up a huge container and empty the garbage into the bin. The smell was potent and the sound from the dumping created a loud thud. That became his image for letting go. The next time he had the urge to stay at work beyond hours, he closed his eyes and recalled the image, along with the sounds and smells. He knew that once he heard and felt the thud of garbage crashing in his body he had purified his emotions of guilt and shame.

Gift Tag

Exercise: Engage Your Senses

Part of purifying your emotions is the engagement of your senses. Imagine the sounds, smells, and sense of touch. Light and sounds keep your vibrations high. For example, you could imagine feeling the wind on your face, or hearing the running water of a stream. The more vibrant your picture, the more likely you will purify the emotion. Here are some more images for letting go: ziplining, leaves falling off a tree, a balloon releasing into the sky, building and wrecking a sand castle, a leaf floating down a stream. Let go of the outcome; you are an emotional being. You are not meant to get rid of your feelings. You are meant to interact with them in a way that builds you up rather than tears you down.

Sound Therapy

Your body is made up of 80 to 90 percent water. Because of this, sounds travel through your body regularly. Joscelyn Godwin, editor of the book *Cosmic Music*, states, "Research has shown that when we are deprived of certain light frequencies we can become sick. One of the most fascinating scientific facts to emerge recently is that sound behaves in a similar fashion to light. In other words, sound and light act like vitamins and minerals in our body . . . We need a certain balance of sound frequencies, which may vary from one individual to another, in order to maintain our bodies in a healthy state."

Certain tones activate your right brain (your conscious mind) and alpha brain wave state. Each of your emotions corresponds and can be measured by frequency. Author Dr. David R. Hawkins reports his research on the subject in his book *Power vs. Force,* where he used techniques such as kinesiology to create a map/scale that came to be known as an emotion calibration chart. In this chart, he was able to pinpoint specific frequencies and vibrations for different emotions. He found that the emotions of love vibrated at approximately 500 hertz. Many people have mistakenly confused love with anguish and worry. Yet worry is a fear-based vibration of only approximately 100 hertz. Here are some other frequencies:

- The Solfeggio sound frequency, also known as 528 hertz, is known to activate the love frequency.
- The 528 hertz frequency is also known as a DNA repair, which means it is highly linked to healing qualities.
- The emotion of guilt may be a 60 hertz. The higher the number, the greater the frequency, which is evidenced by the way you feel. Through advanced technologies, you can now purchase and download these frequencies as a way to shift your state of mind from fear to love. Look for these frequencies on iTunes. Once you find one that works for you, consider listening to it daily (or at least three times per week) for four to six weeks. Keep in mind, these resources do not replace medical treatment.

Other sound therapies like singing, chanting, ringing a Tibetan bowl, and crystal bowl therapy all produce and elevate your vibrations. Sound therapy (provided by a certified sound therapist) balances the body through specialized equipment where various tones and sound waves are produced. These sound waves put you into what is referred to as brain entrainment. They do this by increasing your alpha brain wave state, which is a state where learning and relearning new patterns, beliefs, and thoughts can be more easily achieved. In this case, it would be to teach you how to experience your emotions (in the absence of reactivity) from beginning, to middle, to end. You may experiment with this on your own by using a Tibetan bowl or crystal bowl, both of which produce sound that lasts at a minimum ninety seconds. Some of these sounds can be found through ring tones that you can purchase for your smartphone or on iTunes. You can set an "alarm" so it rings periodically throughout the day. This can be a way to remind and train yourself to pause and breathe.

Gift Tag

Exercise: "Ram"

Ancient traditions reveal that certain sounds when repeated correspond to certain areas of your body. For example, the sound *RAM*, when repeated, vibrates above your navel (solar plexus area). This is the area that typically freezes or depletes energy when you are afraid or worried. By repeating this sound, you are able to not only increase energy but also move it and build your sense of balance and inner strength.

CHAPTER 6

PHASE THREE: HARMONIZE

"No person, no place, and no thing has any power over us, for 'we' are the only thinkers in our mind. When we create peace and harmony and balance in our minds, we will find it in our lives."

—LOUISE L. HAY, *YOU CAN HEAL YOUR LIFE*

The Final Phase

The final phase is to harmonize. This is the process of balancing, integrating, and reinforcing your new state of being. This is the phase that asks you questions such as:

- If you are no longer anxious, what are you?
- Can you picture yourself living without inadequacy, worry, doubt, and fear?
- Can you see yourself in good health, with stamina, vitality, and focus?
- What will you be doing, thinking, and feeling instead?

Picture a snow globe that has been shaken up. Phases 1 and 2 shake up your energy, lifting it up from the bottom, getting it to move and dance around. In Phase 3, the particles are settling down. Your system has been rebooted and now you are learning how to maintain states of balance, harmony, and love. The tools in this section will show you how.

Ritualizing

Rituals differ from routines in that they prepare you from inside out rather than the outside in. Rituals tend to be more rooted in intention (stemming from the heart), whereas routines are focused more on actions, tasks, or duties (carrying out actions of the mind). Rituals are not what you think you should do or what you do because you have to. They are a way to stroke your heart rather than appease the mind. Creating and applying rituals in your life brings you balance.

Rituals can be as simple as beginning each day with a certain stretch, or something you say to yourself. This could be a silent blessing, note of gratitude, or taking a long inhale and exhale. It does not matter what it is—what matters is that you feel it in your heart. Perhaps it is petting your dog, inspirational reading, kissing your child, or listening to the birds. Sarah's rituals were simple, but they had a profound effect on her life.

She had recently lost her father. Although his death wasn't sudden, Sarah hadn't realized the impact it was going to have on her daily functioning. Sarah had always been a type-A person who was able to multitask and juggle many things. Her bouts of sadness made her feel out of sorts, causing her to question how she lived her life. Eventually, due to symptoms of sleeplessness she decided to speak to a professional. She came up with two rituals, one to honor her father and the other to embrace the day. She decided to honor him by kissing his picture and saying, "thanks, Dad." Next, while standing she then put her arms over her head, clasped her hands, and stretched to the right and then to the left, back and forth a few times. She did this daily while moving through the three phases described here and in the previous two chapters. The ritual of kissing and whispering words to her father honored her past, and the stretch represented a way for her to connect to the present moment. This allowed the old energy to move while embracing the new.

Both anxiety and depression benefit from proper breathing, mindfulness, and movement. Again, rituals that connect to your heart will help you integrate your new energy while releasing the old, reinforcing how you choose to live in the now.

Taking Time for Yourself

Living without the negative connections to anxiety will change your relationship with time. Rather than feel as if time is getting away from you, instead you will relish the time you have. You will see this in the choices you make. Your thoughts, behaviors, and attitude will reflect this. To get started you will need to think about what it is you enjoy. What makes you light up and vibrate? If you have been living with anxiety for a long time, this may seem like a difficult question. You may have taken on unconscious and conscious patterns that prevent you from experiencing your true self. Your true self is connected to your most natural states, which include peace, love, balance, and harmony. Anxiety is not your natural state. If you believe this to be true, consider that you have been telling yourself a lie. You know it is a lie, because lies feel heavy and burdensome. Truth feels light and freeing.

If you are a mother of small children or a person who works more than one job, you may feel like moving right through this section. You may say to yourself, *nope, not gonna happen.* Start small. Perhaps for a mother of a newborn, time for yourself is being able to take a hot shower.

When it comes to taking time for yourself, expectations and comparisons often get in the way. For example, you may feel jaded because your neighbor gets to golf all day, or because a single coworker gets to go to the gym daily. If this is the case, by choosing to give yourself permission to dive into the feeling of resentment, jealousy, annoyance, or anger, you will position yourself for freedom. How you presently feel has nothing to do with your neighbor or coworker. There are many people in this world who get to do whatever they want and still have no idea what their natural state is. Try not to compare yourself to others. Instead, find some time for yourself that makes you feel good and works with your lifestyle. People with small children may find that it feels like a mini-retreat just to *be* with your child without becoming caught up in errands and tasks. Now and then, allow yourself to wander and roam into new places. Notice if these places evoke feelings that you have not felt in a while, such as inspiration, enthusiasm, or curiosity. If you feel something new, take it as a sign you are harmonizing. If you tend to revisit the same feelings, then spend more time grounding and purifying, and the harmonizing will come. Other ways to harmonize include pausing (e.g., gazing at the sky), getting outside, playing, going out with a friend, nourishing yourself with healthy foods, reading, napping, keeping a gratitude list, exercising—basically anything that lifts your heart. It is truly how you become who you are and it is from this way of being that you become both a receiver and giver of the gifts.

Merging the Three Phases

Now that you understand the different phases, how they serve you, and the tools for moving through them, it is time to allow these phases to merge into one. The more you practice the tools, the more they just happen, taking on a vibration and culture of their own. You won't have to think so much about what to do next. You will learn to trust that your vibrations uplift you and that the choice to purify and harmonize will always be available. There is no limited supply or deadline you need to reach. If you miss a day or get sidetracked, know opportunities to dive, purify, and ritualize are abundantly around you. So are the lessons, teachable moments, and hints of your gifts.

Gift Tag

Meditation: Round and Round

Picture a Ferris wheel going around and around. Close your eyes and take a long inhale, extending your belly out, and a long exhale, allowing your belly to deflate. Picture your inhale and exhale linking together: on inhale you rise up in the Ferris wheel and on exhale you come down. Feel the motion of energy shifting inside you. See yourself taking in the sights, noises, and nature around you. Feel the wind on your face and skin. You can see the hustle and bustle below; however, you are removed from it at the same time. Where you are, everything is open and free.

Gift Tag

Exercise: Restorative Yoga

Sit down about 6 inches away from a wall, with both your left arm and left leg alongside the wall. Turn yourself so you can lie down on the floor and bring your buttocks close to the wall. As you roll onto your back, lift up your legs straight against the wall. This is referred to as Legs Up the Wall yoga pose. Allow your legs to rest above you comfortably. You may also put a folded blanket underneath you for additional comfort. Allow your arms to rest down by your sides. Close your eyes, separate your lips, and allow yourself to rest for two to three minutes. Allow your breath to move in and out your nose so that your lower belly inflates. Just relax. Not only does this increase circulation in your legs, but it also restores you from your daily grind. This is a great way to harmonize after a long day. You will find it captures all three phases, grounding, purifying, and harmonizing, quite nicely.

PART 3

YOUR GIFTS

You have been a carrier of your gifts since the moment you were conceived. The gifts of purpose, resiliency, empathy, and hope vibrate inside of you. Individuals around you were reflections of the gifts you carry. Your mother, father, caretakers, doctors, and nurses were fed by your existence. You lived and breathed these gifts. Even babies whose lives are tragically cut short transfer gifts into the world. You came in with no attachments, belongings, accomplishments, or expectations. Yet, you managed to stir the energy in others. This included revealing insecurities and fears of those around you. Immediately, you were of service, offering everyone an opportunity to look inside and be healed. The symptoms of anxiety you're now experiencing as an adult are your soul's attempt to call you back to who you are. You have strayed and now it is time to come home.

CHAPTER 7

THE FIRST GIFT: PURPOSE

"Sometimes it's the same moments that take your breath away that breathe purpose and love back into your life."

—STEVE MARABOLI, *UNAPOLOGETICALLY YOU*

Anxiety Focused: Feeling Uncertainty

Gift Focused: Find Your Purpose

Every breath you take has purpose. Breathing not only serves the biological purpose of keeping you alive, but it also cleanses and replenishes your soul's purpose when you are aware of it. It is not uncommon for anxiety to stifle your breath, disconnecting you from the passion that feeds your soul. Individuals in the throes of anxiety symptoms often report being uncomfortable and uncertain. That's because their breathing has been compromised. Anxiety is an abandonment of the breath.

After using the tools in Chapters 4–6, which help you see the symptoms of anxiety in a new way, you'll feel anxiety trying to tell you to pay attention to your breathing. When you pay attention to your breathing, you'll find your purpose. Your breath is the messenger of your inner voice. It may be whispering to you to pause, listen, and notice what is showing up without any fear, preconceived notions, or attachment to where your purpose might lead you. It is also a source to find the courage to be able to look at what triggers your symptoms directly in the eye and say, *I know you, and the stories, beliefs, fears, and memories you are connected to.* It is your breath that allows you to command: *I choose to embrace who you are wholeheartedly for the sake of knowing my purpose.*

Your breath never left you while you were experiencing anxiety, but you might not have been paying attention to it. Your breath has sustained your existence, directed by your mind, waiting patiently in the wings of your lungs for you to raise your vibration and awareness so it can be refurbished, redirected, and anchored by your physical presence.

Pay attention to how your breath speeds up when you are excited, nervous, or invigorated by what is happening around you. Listen to when your breathing feels dull, restless, and empty. Your breathing patterns provide you with inside information about your heart. The patterns will help you identify what you love, what propels you, what you are afraid to look at, and what you may be holding yourself back from. As you open your mind to this information, you will find your purpose and your ability to sustain an intentional life.

Many people want to know what their purpose is. *Why was I created? What's my higher calling?* When you choose to live on with purpose, these insights will be revealed to you. To "live on purpose" means to:

- Notice all of your emotions
- Be mindful of the various ways they are brought to your attention
- Embrace each one

Embracing purpose is not necessarily about achievement or doing something that earns you attention from others. It is to live your life in such a way that you believe every encounter—very often the simplest ones you have with yourself and others—is significant and meaningful. Purpose is not exclusive to encounters with people, but also to how you interact with your environment. In other words, your purpose is how well you are able to pay attention.

Each of your gifts is represented in some way through nature. Watching a bumblebee pollinate can teach you a lot about purpose. For many, purpose comes with a tremendous amount of commitment and dedication. A new mother or father feeding a baby or a student studying for finals can attest to this. Consider the possibility that you were meant to experience the symptoms of anxiety and that you can determine how these symptoms play themselves out. Can you imagine that through the process of receiving your own gifts you could possibly give those around you permission to receive theirs? Is there a greater gift? Can you imagine how it might change the world if everyone recognized and accepted these gifts within themselves? Every war, addiction, and tragedy has an element of fear behind it. You, my friend, have been chosen to shift how anxiety is viewed. Your sensitivity to what is happening around you is what makes you the perfect candidate. All you have to do is activate your purpose by noticing your energy and breathing in what is around you, and the rest will be taken care of.

Notice Your Breath

Your breath brilliantly takes in oxygen and releases carbon dioxide. It distributes all sorts of materials you need (glucose, nitrogen, etc.) throughout your body. Each breath ignites your human experience through emotional shifts. When you are fearful, your breath may contract and pull tight into your body. When you are loving and calm, it expands beyond your skin into the atmosphere. Each breath is unique and significant.

Noticing your breath is a key way to find the gift of purpose. As the value of your breath returns to you, so does your purpose. Choosing to accept this gift grants you:

- Wisdom
- Appreciation
- The ability to listen to your breath

You will notice how each breath sounds, feels, and even tastes different. Some breaths are tinged with roughness while others run smoothly. Some you can feel down in the pit of your stomach, while others spread across your chest, hugging the chambers of your heart.

Like musical notes, each breath has a unique key and pitch. This is the harmony arranged by your mind, body, and spirit.

Each breath carves away at the residue that stress has left behind. With your participation and awareness, your breath will run your purpose through your tissue, bones, and bloodstream. Once again, the tools you learned in Chapters 4–6 will support this process.

Breathing Exercise to Help You Accept Your Gift of Purpose

The following breathing exercise will highlight for you how monitoring your breath brings you closer to your purpose:

1. Take a long deep breath, inhaling and exhaling in and out through your nose. Notice the sound of your inhale and exhale. Notice how it fluctuates and changes, similar to the tides rolling in and out. Some come in with a crash, while others glide across the sand, combing what lies on the surface. Some breaths will be more rhythmic in nature, rising up inside similar to the sunrise, and casting away your worries and doubts at sunset.

2. Now, see yourself joining the process. The old, anxious you might have joined in through sheer will or by self-monitoring your thoughts. Now, you contribute through pictures and visualization. For example, as you create and hear the rough sound in the back of your throat during your exhale, picture your breath scraping away congested energy that may carry traces of unworthiness, guilt, and shame. Imagine the coolness of your inhale as it pushes your abdomen forward, funneling the emergence of your new self.

This process represents the link between you and your gifts. Your physical body supports your connection to the present moment. Your emotions, when in motion, are like oxygen for your soul. Their variations, movement, and changes in frequencies animate the present moment. With your participation, attention, and awareness, your breath and your emotions help you reach the archives of your soul, the space where your gift of purpose resides.

Find Your Purpose Through Your Breath

Sometimes, your purpose might be simply to look at yourself or something significant in your life in a new way. Your purpose can appear in many ways—so don't forget to appreciate the simple parts of your life as well as the complex. Paula's experiences show how this can happen. She had severe food allergies, so she often worried before eating her food. What if somehow the food came into contact with nuts? She worried even if the possibility was next to nothing. Not only did this make it difficult for her to enjoy her food, but it also interfered with her food choices, the amount she ate, the nutrition she received, and her willingness to try new places to eat.

Paula's primary way of handling her fears was to remind herself that it was only her worries that were causing her fears. This appeared to work in the beginning, but over time the symptoms (worries) returned. Paula's therapist recommended she take some time to meditate as a way to become familiar with the shifts that naturally took place in her body. She was told to pay attention to her heartbeat and how her breath changed moment to moment. This suggestion seemed to help too; however, it wasn't until Paula decided to write about her meditation that things truly changed.

Her writings described her meditations in detail, and she found while writing that images and pictures started to pop into her mind. She added this insight to her writings. For example, she wrote how her inhale and exhale appeared as colorful flames that burned off all toxins and impurities that she encountered that day. This visualization encouraged her to alter her self-talk. She decided that instead of telling herself only about her worries, she would give thanks and appreciation to her food.

Writing her meditations down unfolded like the story of a play. Her breath was the main character and her thoughts the storyline. This was a very different experience for Paula, as her thoughts had previously dominated her life. Essentially, she became the source for her own treatment. She learned not only that she had all the answers inside—but also how much her fears held back her appreciation for life. Part of her life's purpose became to appreciate the foods she could eat and what they did for her body.

Connect to Your Higher Self to Find Your Purpose

Your higher self is the embodiment of your vibration and consciousness. It is the part of you that "knows"—you may call it a gut feeling or a sixth sense. The symptoms of anxiety have served you—they were part of your life path, a guidance system for your soul's journey. The symptoms were never the problem; instead, it was how you handled the symptoms that led to anxiety being a burden.

Your anxiety actually helped you by revealing what you truly care about. For example, feelings of self-doubt show you what you are afraid of or have not yet experienced, and fear signals what's holding you back. As you cultivate vibration and embody awareness, your higher self brings forth the clarity and direction you need on your new path. Along the way, your higher self will gently remind you how important it is to take time for yourself, to pause, listen, and focus on the now.

Your higher self is the present moment. It is everything you see, feel, and sense around you. Actually, it is what you can see as well as what you cannot see. You may not be aware that you are interacting with your higher self until after the fact. For example, let's say you baked a cake for a friend. Your friend later tells you that it was the best cake she had ever eaten. Baking up to that point may have been a hobby for you—something you fiddled around with, but never expected to share. Soon your friend tells other friends, and before you know it you are baking a wedding cake for more than 100 people. Could this be a sign that you should go into the cake-making business? Maybe, maybe not. When you connect with something you're passionate about, that's finding your higher self. Having a hobby you enjoy may interrupt negative thinking, instead provoking higher-level thoughts and feelings. While baking the cake you might admire the color and smoothness, the smell of the batter, and your love of cooking. Experiences that keep you in the present moment—sparking your interest, focus, and internal motivation—contribute to the rousing of your higher self.

Your purpose might not be connected to a specific task that you complete. It can be a way that you share your vibration of joy and love. Many people have been taught that they must show evidence of love. For example, a woman may not feel loved if a man doesn't buy her flowers or give her a ring. A man may not feel loved if a woman does not give him attention or sex. Your higher self is the part of you that feels complete, the part of you that knows you are love. How you think, feel, and act influences your love frequency. The emotions of love, peace, joy, and appreciation move freely through your body, carrying a high vibrational frequency. When this occurs you feel hopeful, compassionate, and thankful for the experiences you encounter. When you feel this way, you don't need to look for material evidence of love. You know it exists in you, and you know how to see it in others.

Dr. Masaru Emoto, author of *The Hidden Messages in Water*, found through use of high-speed photography that crystals frozen in water looked different when exposed to both negative and positive thoughts. For example, when the water was exposed to negative thoughts, such as *I hate you* or *you make me sick*, the crystals that formed in the ice made from that water appeared fragmented, disjointed, and dull. When exposed to words such as *gratitude*, *love*, and *peace* the crystals formed beautiful, clear, colorful, and intricate snowflake patterns. Given that "from a physical perspective, humans are water," Emoto determines that "if we have a clear understanding of water, we will better understand the human body." He concludes that purifying this water is the key to living a happy, healthy life.

The symptoms of anxiety were never meant to be controlled; they were meant to be listened to and respected. In fact, the more you try to control them, the less your life flows. Instead, the symptoms are an integral part of your awakening. If your life purpose is to find love, the symptoms of anxiety are there to wake you up, to remind you: *Hey, remember, you are love.* Embracing and allowing yourself to complete your emotions removes any barriers between the incomplete you and your higher self. This clears the way for living a heart-dominated life. Instead of your heart analyzing and evaluating your thoughts, your heart feels, trusts, and deciphers which thoughts are intended to be followed from the ones to breathe into and release.

Similar to someone who is a recovered alcoholic or addict (they can deeply relate), understand and appreciate what it means to live a life "off" anxiety—a clean and sober life. Once you have been held prisoner in your own mind, being able to breathe, expand, and alter how you view your past changes your vibration. With this change comes the unavoidable removal of any limits and boundaries that were placed upon and around your purpose. The following Gift Tag is an exercise for aligning you with who you are. Do this a minimum of one time per day, allowing yourself a minute or two of relaxation once you are done.

Gift Tag

Exercise: Develop Purpose

While sitting in a chair, close your eyes, relax your face, and place your arms by your sides. Begin by taking a few long, deep breaths, inflating your abdomen on inhale and deflating it on exhale. On your fourth breath cycle, begin to notice how your energy feels around you. Pay close attention to the details of your body. Perhaps you can feel your scalp or the hair on your arms. Keep relaxing your jaw, lips, and shoulders.

Now, picture yourself emanating clear, white, or colorful light out into the atmosphere. On your next inhale intentionally state the phrase silently or out loud, *I am limitless*. Toss it out into your energy field like you would a Frisbee or a ball. You can also imagine cupping your hands around your mouth like a megaphone and yelling out to the atmosphere, *I am limitless*. Do this a few times and trust that the electromagnetic energy from your heart (which extends far beyond your brain) is catapulting these words and vibrations into the atmosphere.

Love Yourself to Receive the Gift of Purpose

Love is a high-vibrational energy. The thoughts, feelings, and beliefs you have about your purpose influence these vibrations. If you believe you have to take care of everyone because they are incapable or cannot handle anything without you, your vibrations will reflect this. You may believe that you are motivated by love, but your energy may reflect something different. Worry and fear, when disguised as love, prevent you from trusting in your own purpose as well as the development of purpose in others. (Chapter 11 gives you more information on how to support others.)

Anita Moorjani, author of *Dying to Be Me*, states, "When we know that we are love, we don't need to work at being loving toward others. Instead, we just have to be true to ourselves, and we become instruments of loving energy, which touches everyone we come into contact with." When you respect the energy of your life events, you honor your soul's journey. When you respect the energy of others, you are respecting the process of connecting to your higher self.

You may have learned that love is strong, that it will get you through the tough times and beat all odds. You may have witnessed it through play, family rituals, trials, and hardships. Your choice to receive the gift of purpose gives you permission to focus on and attend to love more than fear. Instead of looking outward and asking, *Who can I trust?* you will look inward and ask, *How can I grow what already exists in me?*

Grow Your Seeds of Love

You have an average of approximately 60,000 thoughts per day. If you use those thoughts in a conscious way to promote love, your purpose will become clearer and clearer. Your awareness of your thoughts not only matures love but purifies it. Emotions and thoughts of bitterness, resentment, and hatred stifle your energy, disconnecting you from your higher self.

Think of your love like a seed. Watering love daily makes it grow. You water it by intentionally choosing what to focus on. You decide ahead of time, before the day has begun, the thoughts, words, feelings, and energy you would like to deepen and amplify. You can do this through affirmations, mantras, prayers, or statements. You are always being presented with choices of fear or love. By choosing to foster love ahead of time, you are less likely to become swayed or motivated by responses of fear. Deb found this out firsthand. She had a best friend who was going through turmoil. Her friend's fiancé had called off her engagement and as a result she was unable to move forward to purchase the home they had planned to buy together. Her present home was sold, so this meant not only a loss of a relationship but also the loss of her home. Deb called her friend to speak to her, and her friend was in tears. She asked Deb what she thought it all meant and what she should do. Deb's voice froze. She wanted to give her friend good, sound advice but found her body guided her to back off and pause rather than speak quickly. It was as if for a moment someone was tugging on the back of her shirt to prevent her from crossing the street without looking. Instead of attempting to find the right words of wisdom, Deb closed her eyes and tuned in to her body. Her friend had started talking again already, and when Deb later did respond, because of her choice to move inward, her thoughts and words were especially compassionate and helpful in nature.

Deb's tight body served as a warning system. It was letting her know that she was about to interrupt her state of love and move toward fear. Had she ignored the signs and pushed her way through, her response may have been tainted. She may have been more likely to judge or attempt to fix the situation. She may have said something like, *Oh, his loss* or *I never felt right about him anyway*. If Deb had said those things, she would have absorbed her friend's negative energy instead of hearing it but responding in a way that was true to herself and her purpose.

Judgments and assumptions tarnish your ability to water the seeds of love. They invalidate the power of embodied love. Deb's body was giving her a clear warning that speaking quickly or attempting to say the right thing may clog her connection to her purpose. By choosing to pause and dive into her fear and uncertainty, Deb can now trust her response will come from her higher self rather than a need to please others.

If you do not water your seeds of love, you may feel small, powerless, limited, controlled by the destiny of others, bitter, and removed from your deepest dreams and desires. You may even begin to believe that your life is falling apart or that you are having a breakdown. Instead of seeing a breakdown, see a breakthrough.

The seeds of love feed your purpose and make sure it, too, grows healthy and strong. You will feel your purpose in how well you pay attention to your own bodily system, receive guidance, and handle the experiences of each day. This includes how you choose to treat memories of the past. Anxiety does not necessarily need you to go to the past, dig it up, and figure out what you need to heal. Your past is right in front of you. It is presented to you through the experiences, encounters, and events of each day. Reflections of your past show up in people, discussions, and relationships. It also shows up in the form of illness, sore spots, or pain. By choosing to promote love over fear, you not only cleanse and purify your past but also inject new memory into these past experiences. By doing so, these memories no longer hold power over you. In the previous example, Deb may have momentarily sensed a memory of fear. Memories of fear are held together by a belief that you are separate from love. By choosing to gather love before speaking, Deb became a creator of her future experiences rather than someone beholden to her past.

Author Pierre Teilhard de Chardin said, "We are spiritual beings having a human experience." You could also say you are a loving being having a human experience. By choosing to step into your purpose you are choosing to let your seeds of love grow. You will find some of your richest fertilizer comes in the form of vulnerability, flow, self-respect, trust, forgiveness, gratitude, and faith.

Gift Tag

Exercise: Affirmation—Let Love Grow

Today, I choose to let love grow. I allow all the experiences that come before me to heal any memories that keep me separate from love. I am love, and today I choose to foster its expansion. I am watering its growth through my self-awareness. My consciousness rather than my self-consciousness is my greatest expression of love. I recognize love as one of my states of creation and honor its affiliation to my purpose.

You Are an Infinite Being

Anxiety makes you see yourself and the situations around you as limited in growth and potential. As a result, you may develop finite beliefs, such as all good things must end, life is unfair, or there is nothing I can do. For many, living a life with anxiety is an unconscious choice to disconnect or separate from their higher self and purpose. When this occurs, your faith becomes unsteady. Purpose and faith are intertwined. As you surrender old patterns and beliefs about anxiety, you will come to see yourself as an endless supply of energy. With that comes the ability to know yourself as an infinite creator of love, forgiveness, and purpose.

The infinite part of you is what connects you to a source. You may call this God, or a higher force. What unites you to this infinite source is consciousness. Accounts and recordings of near-death experiences such as those written by neurosurgeon Eben Alexander (*Proof of Heaven*) and neuroanatomist Jill Bolte Taylor (*My Stroke of Insight*) describe the experience of coming into the infinite part of self in magnificent detail. Both authors send the same profound message: You are more than the physical, and you are intricately connected to something larger.

As you practice increasing your vibrations using the information in the previous chapters, you will come to know yourself as an infinite being. As you do, you will realize that part of your purpose includes transforming and releasing vibrations that no longer serve you. Instead of shrinking with fear, you will know that it positions you toward purpose. The events and emotions that show up in your daily life will no longer be a blockade, but a bridge toward your gifts.

Author Thomas Merton said, "The biggest human temptation is to settle for too little." When you function by thinking in finite ways, you become used to your doubts and fears of failure. Before you know it, you may be habitually engaging in unconscious negative self-talk and judgment. It is when you connect to yourself as an infinite being, part of a source, that this will begin to change. No matter how deep-seated your old fears and doubts are, you can overcome them. Rebecca found that breathing exercises help lead her away from fear and to her infinite being.

Rebecca, a young woman in her mid-twenties, had attempted to take her driver's test two times, but failed. This left her feeling doubtful, insecure, and unworthy. When she was in her teens, she developed an addiction to alcohol and ended up going into treatment. By age twenty, she was clean and sober. Although she had much to be proud of, she continued to carry around the shame she harbored in her earlier years. She finally got the nerve to schedule another driver's test. Her symptoms of worry and anguish came on strong, indicated by her elevated heart rate and nervousness. This time, rather than fret and worry, she decided to connect to her infinite self.

A few days before taking the test, she set the intention to clear any emotions that were getting in the way of her higher potential. She recalled the shame she felt when her family found out she had a drinking problem. Three days before the exam, she closed her eyes for a few minutes and took three deep breaths. On the fourth breath, she visualized the energy of shame funneling down her head, neck, spine, legs, and feet. After a couple of minutes, she sat quietly, observing her breath and noticing the tingly sensation on her skin. She imagined any emotions holding her back releasing into the atmosphere. This release allowed her to connect to her infinite source. She imagined her energy expanding far out into the atmosphere. As she did, she felt lighter and more free. In this new vibration, she pictured herself passing the driver's test with ease. She saw herself being happy and excited.

After five minutes, she wiggled her toes and gently opened her eyes. She felt peaceful and soothed from her connection. The test was no longer the primary focus. Instead, she couldn't help but notice the gratitude and love in her heart.

And yes, she did pass her driver's test.

Gift Tag

Exercise: Affirmation

Say to yourself: *Today I accept myself as an infinite being. As an infinite being, failure and fear do not exist. Love is the only thing that is real.* Repeat this affirmation to yourself whenever you feel disconnected from the gift of purpose.

Return to Love

The gift of purpose comes with the opportunity to get good at love. Anxiety made you good at fear instead. It gives the impression that love has gone away. You probably have a clear understanding of fear from your experiences with anxiety. You know what it looks like, feels like, and how it surfaces in your life. You probably could easily describe how fear affects your thinking, behavior, and relationships. You may have phrases or words that keep it on a tight leash: *I try* or *I can't*. (The words I try are often tied to the energy of struggle or hardship.) Fearful memories and experiences may be easier for you to retrieve than positive ones. Your reaction to fear may slip out quickly, without much contemplation, self-reflection, or awareness. All and all, you have gotten really "good" at fear. Anxiety also gives fear more meaning than love. Yet love is real and is the true carrier for meaning.

Now, through your purpose, you will get good at seeing, feeling, touching, hearing, and noticing love throughout your day. You will pay attention to your thoughts and inner dialogue that are kind and compassionate in nature. Your intention to do so and your awareness of your breath will lead the way. Love will rise up inside you on dark days as well as bright days. You will watch how images of love surface in places you most and least expected it. This mindset can change your life.

Marianne Williamson, the author of *A Return to Love*, states, "Love is what we are born with. Fear is what we learn here. The spiritual journey is the relinquishment—or unlearning—of fear and the acceptance of love back into our hearts." The symptoms of anxiety were a part of your spiritual journey; they led you to an opportunity to experience the return of love.

Undoubtedly, the experience of another's love can be beyond words. It is amazing how children are instantly soothed by the hug of a caregiver. Likewise, there is an inner child in all of us, craving the love, attention, belonging, approval, and affection of another. Without awareness, anxiety can develop into people-pleasing behaviors and a sense of longing for something more. Hallmark cards and romantic movies become a guidepost for what love is rather than your connection to your higher self. When you lose your connection to real love, you can also suffer from a loss of:

- Relationships (the greatest one with your own self!)
- Integrity
- A strong family unit
- Self-esteem
- Your connection to your purpose

Love is an emotion that washes over you like the sun after a long rain. It is the same energy that gives you hope and courage. It is what comes before you smile, hug someone, apologize, make amends, or accept things as they are. The feeling of love can be elicited through memories, sounds, images, movement, creativity, meditation, mindfulness, people, nature, animals, and experiences. It is a sensation that grows from the inside, spreading outward into your extremities. It is capable of pushing aside all your troubles and worries in that moment in time. Individuals who have lost someone close to them often describe experiencing a deep hole in their heart, an aching from missing someone so much. This is a sign that their bodies have stored warm, heartfelt memories from the experience of a deep love. Relationships and people can enhance the love that exists in you. It may appear that they have given this love to you; however, it is likely it actually magnified the love already inside you. If this were not the case, then love would be limited in supply and temporary.

Many have mistakenly attempted to fill their emptiness with love from another source. Relationships, food, sex, and material possessions may serve as a temporary surrogate for true love. Many who struggle with anxiety focus on the flaws and disappointments of others—this is often a projection of their own insecurities and fears. These projections sometimes surface as anger, jealousy, and blame. (You may recall witnessing such projections as a child.) Hurtful exchanges give the impression that love is something to be manipulated, used, or taken away. As a result, you may have learned that fear is more real than love.

Accessing the gift of your purpose will help you relearn love and surrender your fear. As this occurs, the meaning of your purpose strengthens and becomes clear. This cycle of and connection between love and purpose will make your life grow rich, as both your inner and outer worlds expand. Love is abundant and, when permitted, will bless you beyond what you ever expected. As you unlearn fear and tune into love, you will realize there is plenty of goodness to go around. Accept it is yours.

The following Gift Tags are exercises for cultivating your relationship with love. Anxiety when maintained numbs your senses. Part of your purpose is to reinvigorate them. As you do you will be able to breathe love into different situations.

Gift Tag

Exercise: Recipe for Increasing Love

Here are the ingredients you'll need: your body, an awareness of your breath, gratitude, focus, sensations, and your five senses (touch, sound, vision, taste, smell).

- Walk and talk more slowly, mindfully placing one foot in front of the other.
- Now and then, pause between words when you speak.
- Take three deep breaths once an hour.
- Consider closing your eyes for a moment when parked in your car.
- Check in with your heart by observing the breath in your body.
- Take a new route to work to keep your senses fresh. Practice gratitude.

Gift Tag

Exercise: Center Yourself

When your heart is in balance (meaning your energy is in flow), you feel centered. Connecting to your center is a way to nourish your love. The best way to do this is to connect to the energy of the earth. Go outside and notice, sense, and feel earthly treasures such as rocks, soil, water, sand, crystals, leaves, sticks, and more. Hold them in the palm of your hand while breathing deeply. Walk barefoot while taking in the images around you. Pay attention to sounds and signs of love, perhaps a bird chirping or gathering food for his babies. Notice how forgiving nature is. After a harsh, long winter, the grass still turns green, flowers bloom, and leaves grow. Imagine transferring this same forgiving energy into your heart. You may even say to yourself while breathing, I breathe in love, I breathe out fear. Do this exercise as often as you can, using the treasures from your own environment. It not only clears away past hurts—it also helps you enhance and memorize love.

Find Truth

Truth is not something you obtain, but rather an experience of your energy in motion. Instead of seeking truth or distancing yourself from it by attempting to figure it out, accept that truth has already occurred. You came into the world in your truth. Each time you breathe, smile, laugh, offer an act of kindness, such as holding the door open for someone, or notice the good around you, you are experiencing truth. The truth is you came into existence on purpose and to serve. You can see truth in the moments you give space to your imperfections, knowing they bring you just the right amount of vulnerability to melt your perceived obstacles.

Rather than pulling your energy tight as if you were pulling on a too-small pair of jeans, release the energy so you can breathe. When you quit attempting to fit in, you can see truth. Truth happens each time you offer gratitude, pet your dog, feel the temperature on your skin, soften your gaze, and truly taste your food. Truth is when you say goodnight to the moon, good morning to the sun, notice the shadows, plant a flower, and catch a glimpse of the stars in the sky.

Many people pray for their lives to change, to gain peace in their hearts, or for the healing and well-being of another. It is rare to hear someone say that she is praying and asking for truth. The fact of the matter is, truth might be the very thing you are afraid of. By keeping it at a distance, you may find your love can only stretch so far. At some point, in order to sustain and deepen the gift of purpose, you will need to reach into your soul and be willing to have an intimate experience with truth.

In your mind, you may think, *I don't want to know,* or view the process as painful. You are human, and it is natural to want to avoid pain. In fact, it is how your ancestors before you survived. One of the truths the human race now faces is that humanity has changed. The symptoms once designed to warn our ancestors about potential danger from predators in the wilderness have taken on new meaning in modern life. They are a signal that you have disconnected from your body and soul, the place where your higher self resides. This is where your truth is housed—and kept secret from your conscious mind. By choosing to ignore its existence, you are electing to manage the symptoms of anxiety rather than allowing them to guide you to freedom.

On the outside, you may see yourself improving. This is a sign of your truth beginning to emerge. Perhaps you have lost weight, are making healthier choices, or are taking more time for yourself. However, without fully engaging your body in a way that stimulates your subconscious mind, you may find yourself easing back into old, familiar patterns. True transformation happens when the whole you steps forward—not just the physical, nor just the emotional or spiritual, but the entire makeup of your mind, body, and soul. If you wade into the water only up to the lower half of your body and never get the rest of yourself wet, you aren't really swimming. Likewise, you won't find truth by just wading in; you must dive under.

The process of evoking truth requires four things:

1. Being willing to ask for it to be revealed
2. Focusing on the questions more than the answers
3. Allowing yourself to become familiar with, digest, and pass the emotions that show up
4. Noticing how truth and love are connected

The Dalai Lama said, "The more you are motivated by love, the more fearless and free your actions will be." Dwelling on love versus fear opens up the pathway to truth. In order to do this, it will be important for you to connect to your body in a new way. You will learn the value of dwelling in a body free from the negative interpretations of anxiety. Re-educating yourself about truth will assist you in this process. Many people avoid truth because they have been conditioned to see it as a quest for fault finding. To do so would highlight your wrongdoings: the mistakes, screwups, or ways you have hurt others or messed up your life. You have connected truth to weakness and lack—both of which contribute to the belief that you are not enough.

Truth has nothing to do with lack. As an infinite being, you are perfect. The soul does not judge you. Let me repeat, the soul does not judge you. In fact, when you judge or fear your truth, you disconnect from the force that brings you peace. You might refer to this force as the holy spirit or the universal life force. The voice inside your head that tells you it is not safe to face truth is your fear. The truth is light and when you encounter it, you actually feel lighter. Fear, on the other hand, is heavy, paralyzing, and dark.

Ask for Your Truth to Be Revealed

Before asking for your truth to be revealed to you, it will be important for you to notice the moments you feel light. Notice the times in your day when you feel open, receptive, and more able to breathe consciously. If breathing continues to be a challenge for you, consider doing the tapping technique (Chapter 4). Tap the side of your hand (halfway between the bottom of your pinky and wrist) and while breathing in through your nose and out through your mouth, say to yourself, *Even though I feel I can't breathe, I completely love myself.* Tap anywhere from one to four minutes. Close your eyes and see the belief that you cannot breathe travel down your spine in the form of light. This light represents truth. The truth is, you are breathing and you are loved. Once you are done tapping, sit quietly, close your eyes, and notice the space in between your ribs, in your abdomen and chest. Allow yourself to submerge into this space.

Asking truth to reveal itself can be done during meditation, as a form of prayer, or as a way to speak to your higher consciousness before you go to sleep. It can be as simple as, *Higher consciousness, please show me my truth. Thank you.* The serenity prayer in many ways is a truth prayer and has helped so many people through some of the darkest times. This too may be a way to ask for truth:

> *God, grant me the serenity to accept the things I cannot change, the courage to change the things I can, And the wisdom to know the difference.*

Once you have asked for truth, consider your request heard. Trust and know that truth will show up; however, it might not always be in the way you expect it. Simply observe and notice who and what shows up in your day without judgment. Sometimes truth shows up in the form of what you hate. What you hate is certainly not your truth, but it can block it. What you dislike may harbor a feeling that if permitted to be experienced will set you free. For example, if you hear yourself say, *I hate surprises*, then perhaps the feeling of shock is something you need to acknowledge, breathe into, and allow to flow off your back.

Other times, truth will show up as a symbol, a declarative statement in your head, through another individual, an experience, or a feeling. You may hear something like, *Wait*, or *Everything will be okay*. You do not need to hunt for truth, just observe and allow it to arrive. If you feel closed off or judgmental, that may be an indication that you still have something to experience—perhaps an old emotion, belief, or act of forgiveness—before truth can appear. If you feel light and open, soak up and relish that sensation.

Ask Questions

The second part of evoking truth is to focus more on asking yourself questions than on finding the right answers. Wanting to know why things are as they are can block your connection to truth. Remember, you already have the answers inside of you. Instead, ask questions that provoke reflective thinking and spark feeling. Contrary to what you may believe, feeling is a pain reducer. Thinking, on the other hand, when overused, can create an emotional buildup of blockages that may develop into aloofness, physical pain, and, at times, illness. The answers will come, but they will develop from feeling, and because of this they will be more intuitive in nature. In the long run, this is a more productive way to handle the energy of your emotions.

Author and psychiatrist Keith Ablow states in *Living the Truth*, "All of us develop . . . 'shield strategies' to keep emotional pain at bay." His book recommends reflecting on thoughts or questions such as:

- I want people to know how _____ I am because ____.
- My shield strategy is_____(e.g., staying on the computer for hours).
- What part of your life story as a child or young adult took the most strength to survive?

As you reflect on thoughts such as these, consider marinating in the emotional energy that gets stirred. You may feel energy seep into the tops of your shoulders or your neck. Close your eyes and breathe into it. Beyond the tension is your truth. If you have ever given birth to a child, the process is similar. At first you notice and feel the pain and then at some point, you have to reach in deep and find your breath. You do this because the experience could not be more real. It is one of the most raw, vulnerable, tender, and miraculous human experiences. In that moment, what is happening is much bigger than the four walls of that room. Not only is a child born, but also a soul. The lives he or she will touch and impact is a depiction of truth.

Let Your Emotions Pass

The third step is to respect and pass sensations that arise. When congested, heavier energy does arise, so take a moment and pause for thirty to sixty seconds. Remember the phases you learned in Chapters 4–6. These are your guideposts for experiencing your feelings and increasing your vibrations. Emotions are part of your human experience. Fear will show up as needed—the difference will be in how you handle it as well as how easily you revert back to truth. If you choose to focus on your progress more so than your setbacks, you will return faster.

Truth and Love Are Connected

The final step to evoking your truth is noticing how truth and love are connected. Truth shows itself through opportunities to experience your own love. Your love can break through old, congested emotions and beliefs to create opportunities for inner growth. Your history with anxiety was most likely physiological and psychological in nature. Your future without it will be an integration of your mind, body, and spirit. This is your truth and your gift of purpose.

Gift Tag

Reflection: Goose Bumps

Do you remember a time that you suddenly got goose bumps or the shivers, perhaps after hearing a story? This could be a sign that you were encountering something that resonated with your truth. It could be your intuition telling you something or reinforcement of what you already know.

CHAPTER 8

THE SECOND GIFT: RESILIENCY

"Happiness is not a matter of intensity but of balance, order, rhythm, and harmony."

—THOMAS MERTON, AUTHOR

Anxiety Focused: Experiencing Powerlessness

Gift Focused: Become Resilient

Anxiety is like a fever. Some days it wipes you out completely, robbing your ability to withstand, connect to, and appreciate life. Other days, it is similar to a low-grade fever—you may still be able to go about your day, but you feel disjointed, achy, tired, and out of sorts. As you learn and practice working with rather than against the symptoms, your second gift of resiliency begins to emerge.

What Is Resiliency?

There are numerous definitions for resiliency. Dr. Romeo Vitelli offers this one in *Psychology Today*: "The process of, capacity for, or outcome of successful adaptation despite challenging or threatening circumstances." In the context of this book, what makes one person more resilient than another is dependent on many factors. Much research on resiliency has come from studying individuals who have encountered unexpected traumatic experiences, such as an earthquake or hurricane. Individuals who have endured negative environments or traumas, such as child abuse, have also contributed a great deal to research. The findings so far have been inconsistent, as some victims of abuse can at times display stronger resiliency than those who have not. What researchers do agree on is that resiliency can be taught, and rather than focusing on who is more resilient and why, it may be best to focus on how you can become resilient.

Some of the "how" comes from cognitive therapists. They emphasize these tactics as effective for promoting resiliency:

- Practicing stress-reduction techniques
- Sharpening problem-solving skills and
- Altering counterproductive thoughts and beliefs

How you view the symptoms of anxiety in yourself (as well as in others) influences the development of this gift. As stated earlier in the book, you are already resilient. If you were not, you would not exist on earth. Solidifying your understanding of the ego, what it does for you, and ways to re-educate it helps you to tap into your existing resources.

What Is Your Ego?

The analytic concept of the ego was first introduced by the famous psychoanalyst Sigmund Freud. It refers to your identity—the image you uphold of yourself. It is how you see yourself and also your conception of how others see you. Here are some characteristics of the ego:

- Your ego does not like change. It is your protector, and sees change as a potential threat to your survival.
- Its loyalty secures your beliefs, even if they do not serve you.
- The ego believes your worth is based solely on your appearance, possessions, and accomplishments. It is the inner voice that calls you fat, old, and bald. It is also the part of you that cares how many likes your Facebook profile has.
- Its investment is in showing you your outer world, even if it is skewed by your inner emotions.
- The ego pushes you to avoid pain at all costs. This is great if you are about to touch a hot stove or if you are surviving in

the wild. However, if you just lost your best friend or parent, that response could be detrimental to your well-being.

- It is the inner voice that judges you, reminds you to toughen up, and alerts you to be on guard for weaknesses. For someone who is about to enter a race or a competition, this may be helpful. However, when your ego seeps into your second grader's soccer game or you find yourself yelling at slower cars in the church parking lot, it is a lot less helpful.

- It is the voice that reminds you of how alone and separate you are from others. It can even prevent you from seeking assistance from others. It is the part of you that says, *Screw them; they aren't worth my time, I'm not going to a shrink,* or *That person is just out to get me.* The ego is paranoid. Again, this could be beneficial if there were something you truly needed to be warned about—but in modern times, that's not usually the case.

- The ego is the presenter of limitations. It is the part of you that procrastinates and ruminates over possible scenarios and outcomes. It loves to predict outcomes and truly believes it can. When the outcome just by chance does occur, the ego is the first to say, *I told you so.*

- The ego is very attentive to stereotypes and judgments. It is the part of you, your inner child, that reminds you of myths like boys don't cry, girls play nice, and perfect families really do exist. The ego says things like *I'll never, I should,* or *What if?* Without that parrot on your shoulder, taking a leap of faith would not feel nearly as good.

- The ego is a time watcher. It takes pride in being first and keeps close watch on those who are late. If you are a manager or business owner, the ego can help you keep things in check. The challenge is that when you want to turn it off at the end of the day, the ego keeps running.

- It is a lover of lists and tasks. It is that little voice that says once you get it all done, you can relax . . . or maybe not.

How to Re-Educate Your Ego

When misunderstood, the ego can be a nuisance and barrier to growth. However, when you truly grasp the ego—how it attempts to help you as well as the ways it does not—it becomes your ally. Its loyal, persistent qualities can work in your favor. As you allow yourself to feel unfinished emotions and clear self-limiting beliefs, you begin to implant new emotions and beliefs. The new ones are more aligned with your truth and, therefore, your soul. The ego then becomes a reinforcer for instilling and preserving your gifts rather than your fears. The following outlines the steps:

Five Steps to Re-Educating Your Ego

1. Recognize it is your ego (e.g., become aware of when you feel pressure).
2. Allow yourself to experience any unfinished emotions (close your eyes and breathe through them).
3. Ask yourself what self-limiting beliefs are coming up for you right now (e.g., times you say to yourself, *I will never . . .*).
4. Breathe love into these beliefs (think instead, *I am grateful for . . .*).
5. Replace them with a new belief (e.g., think instead, *Everything works out for me*).

Listen to Your Heart over Your Ego

Resiliency happens when the wisdom of your own heart and the comfort of your own body are more pronounced than the voice of the ego. You might find that you have a situation like Susan's, which was alleviated by the five-step process of re-educating the ego. Susan had three sisters. She had a good relationship with two of them, but had trouble with the oldest. When she spoke on the phone with her oldest sister, she always found herself defending or explaining herself. She felt that her sister always took things personally or only saw the negative in the situation. As a way to cope, she would rarely call, and although she knew this hurt her sister, she did not see an alternative.

Once Susan learned about the ego and applied the previous five steps, her attitude began to shift. She realized that her ego was attempting to protect her from hurt and pain. However, it was not doing a great job, as she also felt unsupported in other areas of her life. It showed up at home with her husband and children, and occasionally at work. Carrying these feelings created a tremendous amount of worry, which she attempted to control through *doing* rather than *feeling*.

Susan decided to re-educate her ego:

1. She began by recognizing that her ego was attempting to protect her from pain and preserve her identity as a strong woman who did not need anyone.
2. Next, she sat quietly in a chair, put her feet on the floor, closed her eyes, took a few deep breaths, and asked her higher self to reveal a self-limiting belief or emotion contributing to her anger, frustration, and fear around her oldest sister. She then paused and breathed.
3. As she allowed her mind to relax and her body to vibrate, a few beliefs surfaced, such as *No one supports me* and *I am all alone*. She also felt some sadness surface. Next, she released her jaw and allowed herself to relax as she breathed the energy of her love into these beliefs and emotions. She could feel her breaths deepen and shift from high up in

her chest across her shoulders and neck. As she relaxed, her breath was able to travel deeper into her lower abdomen. To assist the process, she imagined a flock of birds flying freely.

4. Finally, she asked herself what new belief or emotion she wanted to instill. *I am supported* and *I am loved* came to mind. At first, saying these new statements felt a bit awkward and fake. She continued to repeat them to herself during a quiet moment of her day, once a day for a couple of weeks. After a while, she could feel the vibration of the words in her body. She still continued to set limits on how often she spoke with her sister; however, when they did talk, she felt less rattled. The next step for Susan would be to notice other areas of her life where she could also make this shift.

The people you may feel most judged or hurt by often reveal your deepest wounds. To rehash the story behind this pain without support may be overwhelming and in some cases unnecessary. However, acknowledging your ego and choosing to re-educate it is a way to build your inner resiliency. Once again, the phases in Chapters 4–6 were applied to the previous situation. As a result Susan became more comfortable in her own skin.

Fill Yourself Up

Resiliency is the ability to begin from your wholeness rather than your journey to reach it. To be whole means you are flawless and complete. It is not about being better, nor is it an attempt to repair what you consider to be damaged. When you approach resiliency from a place of negativity, you are coming from a low vibration. This makes it very difficult—at times exhausting—to pick yourself up, feel better, and make more compassionate choices. Allowing yourself time to move through the symptoms of anxiety brings forth this gift.

What Does It Mean to Be Filled Up?

Part of the process of learning how to fill yourself up is understanding the difference between your ego and your soul. The ego, housed energetically in your solar plexus (which is located two inches above your navel), comes from low energy when triggered before your heart. When this occurs, you may seek power and control. Learning to redirect your energy to come from your heart is a way to make a connection to your soul. Your heart, when permitted to clear past hurts, beliefs, and emotions, filters and magnifies perceptions through a lens of love. Its electromagnetic field is up to sixty times greater than the one around your head (brain). Higher-vibrational states, such as love, radiate out from your heart similar to a radio transmitter. Being able to sense and feel this extension of yourself (beyond your physical body) fills you up. Not only do you benefit from being filled with higher vibrational energy, but it is likely that you will also send out love into the world around you. This means you become the bridge or the doorway between both giving and receiving love.

Redirect Your Energy Through Pauses

Your ego may have convinced you that things—more time, money, or people—could fill you up. However, your soul knows you are already complete and will not comprehend the ego's approach. Your body is the vehicle to your soul. It is your tether to the present moment and perfectly designed through its intricate anatomy (lungs, heart, sense, right- and left-brain connections, energy systems) to move energy from your heart around your body and into the world.

One of the simplest and most powerful ways to redirect energy is to incorporate more pauses into your day. Pauses are the space between thoughts, words, actions, and movement. Pauses not only create space; they are the gaps between you and your soul. If you hold your breath for a moment, you may notice your solar plexus contract. It feels similar to how you breathe when doing a sit-up. However, if you breathe and inflate your lower belly, you will notice how your breath travels into your solar plexus, heart, and throat. Pauses that contract your abdomen and never allow your breath to expand and circulate may short-circuit your energy. On the other hand, pauses that allow the extension of your belly and the circulation of your breath stimulate energy. Consider trying both approaches and notice which one makes you feel more open, lighter, and thus resilient. Imagine if someone asked you to help her move her couch. In your mind, you may think, *Oh, I am not in the mood to lift something heavy*. When you go over to her house, you realize the couch is lighter than you imagined and quite easy to maneuver. Inside, you feel a sense of relief and leave feeling good that you were actually able to help. Imagine having these types of experiences over and over again. Soon your brain and body would become more open to different types of experiences. Things, situations, or people that formerly triggered reactivity no longer would. Pausing more throughout your day to receive your own energy gives you a sense of fullness. This decreases the chances of life's challenges turning into a conveyer belt of lost energy and instead builds your resiliency.

Reduce Stress by Filling Up

Filling up can help you in everyday situations when you encounter anxiety. For example, Paul worked for a company that held meetings once a month on a Friday afternoon. He hated these meetings and frequently found himself complaining about them days before. As a result, he often showed up at the meeting irritated and annoyed, which was reflected in his overall body language and sarcasm. Frustrated and unhappy, Paul decided to try filling up before the meeting. Since he had a habit of ruminating about the meeting hours before, he set the intention to take the time to pause more throughout his day. For example, after lunch instead of rushing back to his office, he took a moment outside to breathe and take in the day. The wind was blowing and as he watched the leaves rustling, he imagined all the energy that he had leaked throughout his morning returning to him. With his arms by his side, he turned his palms outward, giving the signal to his mind and body that he was choosing to receive. After a few minutes, he noticed that he could actually feel his heart beating and feel his breath rising and falling. At one point, another coworker approached him. Normally, he would get annoyed and think that person was stealing his time to pause. Yet the ritual of committing to this practice daily changed how he viewed interruptions. With practice, his ability to fill up became stronger and less dependent on time. Within a couple of months, he found he was able to receive the benefits in less than one minute. This altered not only how he approached the meetings (he became more upbeat and tolerant), but also his attitude toward others.

Gift Tag

Exercise: Re-Educate Your Ego

The ego is the voice that reminds you of what you need to fix or what could go wrong. Take advantage of a full moon on a clear night. Go outside and take in its vastness, beauty, and full light. This is your image for wholeness. See, sense, and feel this image in your body. Re-educating your ego is the process of engaging your senses while increasing your emotional vibration. While imagining the full moon, you may later repeat an affirmation such as: *I accept my wholeness completely and freely.*

Listen to Your Intuition

Caroline Myss said, "Intuitive skill is being recognized as our most powerful sensory ability." Intuition is the ability to understand something immediately without conscious reasoning. Intuition happens when you don't necessarily have the physical evidence for what it is you know, but you just do, and this brings you a sense of comfort and peace.

Your conscious mind is what you tap into when you reason, make decisions, problem solve, and act off instinct. It makes up approximately 10 percent of who you are. The remaining 90 percent is a blend of your subconscious mind (things not presently in your awareness but that affect you) and intuition. Anxiety, when misunderstood, suppresses this part of you. As a result, you may second-guess, doubt, and become frustrated with things that occur in your life. This pushes you to judge, analyze, blame, and overfocus on what is happening around you.

Your intuitive self is the part of you that trusts what is happening as a guidance system toward your gifts. Resiliency is your ability to maintain a state of flow no matter what happens. In this state, you are able to sense, feel, hear, and trust that what you see and whom you encounter are all reflections of something greater.

The Connection Between Resiliency and Intuition

Your conscious mind may point out the limitations and obstacles you must overcome to live a life free from the negativity that anxiety can bring. Your intuitive higher mind, however, knows your situation will not last forever. It believes in your innate goodness and is open to the possibility that your evolution is steered by forces greater than you. Not only are you being guided, but also you are a source of guidance for others. Without realizing it you may be a symbol, messenger, teacher, well of inspiration, or even a distraction. You may have been purposefully positioned to stumble upon the life path of another. In many cases, you were positioned as a carrier of the gifts. The stronger your connection to your gifts, the more viable and open you become to your service. Perhaps your resiliency played a role in the life of another. Everything in your life is significant. Knowing and accepting this as truth gives the gift of resiliency deeper meaning and value. Intuition can be a wellspring for resiliency because intuition breeds acceptance for the present moment and offers you an opportunity to surrender control. Embracing the symptoms of anxiety as potential sources of vibration fuels this part of you. For example, if you were to schedule an important business meeting and the other party did not show up, consciously you may attempt to understand why she did not show. Your mind may go in many directions trying to figure out if she changed her mind, if something happened on the way to the meeting, or if you might have lost a potential customer. As you strengthen your intuition, these types of situations will not be as likely to rattle you.

Everyone has intuition. It's like a muscle, however—you have to exercise it to make it stronger. Practices that strengthen your connection to the present moment build this skill. Your mind will try to question everything and become consumed with time, details, and outcomes. However, when you tune into intuition, you develop a faith that everything happening around you is intricately designed to help you access your gifts.

How to Strengthen Intuition

Just like resiliency, you can practice tuning in to your intuition. The more often you do that, the stronger your connection to it will become. Then, you'll be more likely to turn to intuition instead of your ego in moments of doubt or uncertainty. Three ways to develop your intuition are to: understand the difference between instincts and intuition, connect to the present moment, and practice humility. Let's look at each in more detail.

Understand the Difference Between Instinct and Intuition

Your **instincts** are more reflexive in nature. They can be based on a hunch; for example, you may have a sense of what someone might say or do. You can also sense when there is tension in a room based on instinct.

Intuition, on the other hand, is an inner knowing. It's often described as an awareness or connection to a higher intelligence. It is an energy that may be experienced as creativity or as a moment of awareness. It may be as simple as a word, image, or encounter that has left an impression on you. For example, you may have a job that pays the bills and supports your family, but there is an inner nudge that says there are other opportunities in store for you. There are many accounts of individuals who have successfully built careers in one area but through creative exploration received an inner knowing that their passion and resiliency resided in another.

Practice noticing the times when your thoughts and actions are based more on instinct. (Perhaps you feel the pressure of family and work.) Instead of experiencing how it settles in your body, you (instinctively) push it away through your thoughts and fears. Noticing how and where it settles in your body allows you to feel (intuitively) and receive the support and reassurance of your own inner guidance.

Connect to the Present Moment

Research shows that when you experience intuition, both the right side of your brain and the prefrontal cortex are activated. These are the same areas that influence your behaviors, motor functioning, and your connection to the here and now. Many people associate intuition with the ability to forecast the future or tap into the records of the past. Try to ignore those associations. Stay committed to the intention of connecting to your gifts, nothing else. Agendas and attachment to wanting to prove or disprove your intuitive abilities can take you off track of your goal, which is to find the gifts of anxiety. Here are some ways to stay in the moment:

- Taking five minutes a day to close your eyes and witness your breath without judgment strengthens your ability to live in the moment. You may find going outside and doing something you love such as fishing, biking, boating, yard work, or gardening, helps you to do this. In addition, pay attention to coincidences or synchronicities throughout your week or day.
- Look for unexpected signs and symbols that validate your intuition.
- Make a conscious effort to observe and incorporate more pauses into your day.
- Engage your senses and refrain from using substances such as alcohol and drugs that alter them.
- See situations that slow you down (e.g., traffic) as opportunities to delve into the moment where you can make conscious contact with your intuition.

Practice Humility

There is a strong relationship between developing humility and your gift of resiliency. Humility is your ability to see and sense worthiness in others and in your environment. Observing worthiness requires a deep ability to feel and listen. Listening and feeling are the same skills exercised for strengthening intuition. How you listen not only to others but also to *your* thoughts and bodily responses can either build you up or hold you down.

For example, notice the energy in your body as you prepare to take on something challenging like an assignment, busy day, or an appointment you are dreading. Do you armor up by protecting rather than feeling your feelings? How will you know if this is happening? Very often, your body will speak to you, offering you feedback through tightness in your neck or shoulders. If you allow yourself a moment to quiet your mind by noticing your body and breath (without expectation or judgment), something magical can happen: you'll feel your intuition.

Intuition is a higher knowing that happens from a relaxed energy. It is an inner trust that communicates beyond the world you can see. Intuition is what tells you everything is going to work out fine. As you learn to trust the inner workings of your body, you become more humble. You recognize that each person and situation in your life is the perfect reflection for how you are experiencing your gifts. You may not always agree with the words or choices of another; however, your interpretation of others will be based less on their words, actions, and appearance, and more on their energy. By focusing on the energy of others instead of what they lack, you will better understand your own energy, the way you can change it, and most of all how it influences others.

Author Dr. Wayne W. Dyer says in *The Power of Intention*, "When you meet anyone, treat the event as a holy encounter. It's through others that we either find or love our self." Some of the most humble moments are when you stop looking to others to change and instead choose to look at yourself. Humility is when you see an aspect of someone else that is underdeveloped in you or a reminder of how well you have fostered certain qualities in yourself (without judgment). Rather than getting angry, arrogant, or envious, you see each encounter as a lesson, even if it was minor or brief. The symptoms of anxiety may direct you to focus primarily on yourself. Let's say you run into a certain person you haven't seen much lately a few times during the course of a week. At first it may seem like a coincidence, but by the third time you begin to wonder if the universe is sending you a message.

Your intuition kicks in—not what you think but how you feel. Sometimes it can feel odd or interesting.

Humility maintains your service on this planet. Your service is not just about what you do, but who you are. You serve even when you are alone and no one is looking. Your thoughts and intentions send out a powerful vibration. Mindful acts such as turning off or ignoring your cell phone when speaking to another individual, volunteer work, and prayer are ways to bring your service to others. If you are always tied up or distracted this turns off your intuitive antennas. Actions such as recycling your items and respecting nature's resources breed deep appreciation, which in turn cultivates humility. Your ability to connect with others will serve you in countless ways throughout your life. Glossing over someone's feelings can have difficult consequences, as Marybeth discovered.

Marybeth was a primary care physician. A woman in her fifties came to see her for an annual exam. Marybeth noticed immediately that the woman did not seem as upbeat and open as usual. She commented to the woman that she seemed a bit off. The woman agreed that she had not been feeling like herself. Immediately, Marybeth spoke about the possibility of prescribing her an antidepressant. The woman took great offense, and said, "How dare you try to fix my emotions? By respecting my feelings, you respect me." Immediately, Marybeth apologized and agreed that her actions were robotic in nature. She assumed this was what the woman would want since so many of her patients seemed to choose this route.

Gift Tag

Reflection: Listening or Directing?

Ask yourself, *Where and with whom in my life have I lost sight of a person and instead focused on the task at hand?* Consider times when you may have been more attached to giving the order rather than listening to the information. How might your intuition have served you in those moments?

Recognize Your Support System

Strengthening intuition increases your support system. Many people feel as if they don't have much of a support system when they're dealing with anxiety. That's because the symptoms of anxiety may be an indication of a subconscious belief that you are a burden—that somehow you don't deserve to ask for help, or that doing so would be a sign that you are weak. As a result, family and friends around you receive mixed messages about your needs and desires. You may seem overwhelmed, but then refuse help.

Fear (which anxiety breeds) pushes people energetically away, whereas love draws them closer. If someone has hurt you and is living an unhealthy life, to the point that they are no longer conscious of their actions toward others, it will be important for you to ask for spiritual guidance.

Where Is Your Support System?

You have many sources of guidance in the physical realm, including people, community, and nature. You also have sources of guidance in the spiritual realm, including guides, masters, and angels. If you have been relying exclusively on what you can see from the 10 percent of your conscious mind, you are neglecting the abundance of love and support available to you. Strengthening your connection to your energy exposes you to more abundance and love than you could ever fathom. Consider that the symptoms of anxiety have brought you to this point. They are a constant reminder of all that you have and are, rather than what you lack.

Embracing resiliency opens up your mind to the possibility that your support system extends far beyond what you know.

Have you ever felt touched by an experience? For example, maybe an unexpected person gave you a gift or told you how much you helped her in some way. Perhaps someone trusted you with one of her deepest fears or took the extra time to reach out to you in a kind way. Now imagine someone tells you how special or helpful you are and your response is, *It was no big deal* and then you change the subject. These types of responses push high-vibrational energy away, never really allowing you to fully embrace the various types of support that come your way. When you choose to fully receive and soak up the compliment by pausing in the moment and perhaps returning the same beautiful energy with a smile, you have connected to the spiritual realm. The spiritual realm is not just a place you might believe you go when you die; it is an energy of grace brought to you through the experiences and encounters that you are willing to notice and receive. You may pray for what you want; however, the way your desire shows up may not necessarily be as you imagined. For example, perhaps you asked for peace and the person who told you how much they appreciated you was sent your way. Hearing her words would mean a great deal, but you might not immediately connect it to peace. If you reflect on the energy accompanied by the words, it could have very well been your request for peace being answered.

Your support system goes far beyond what you can see. It does not matter whether or not you have been practicing a certain religion—the spiritual realm is available to you. What matters is that you exist and thus it is your birthright not only to receive this support but also to ask for it.

How to Ask for Help

Believe it or not, there is a skill to asking for help. The Gift Tag at the end of this chapter will help you learn the art of communicating with your soul. Keep in mind that the soul does not keep tabs on time. Therefore, when you ask for assistance, it is important for you to speak from the present moment. Digging into the past or thinking of the future muddies your emotional waters.

There are four things to keep in mind when asking for help:

1. State your request in the present tense, as if it is already being given.
2. Give the spirit permission to help you.
3. Give yourself permission to receive help.
4. Give thanks and detach from the outcome.

Try not to expect your support to show up in a certain way. It may not look at all like what you expected. Many times, you may receive the awareness of a belief or emotion that needs to be cleared before what it is you are asking for can arrive. Trust that it is all being orchestrated for you.

Here's an example of someone following those four steps to solve a common problem. Molly was terrified of public speaking. When she needed to make a presentation or answer a question in front of even a small group, she could feel the onset of symptoms such as redness in her face, increased heart rate, and nervousness. Her job required her to participate in board meetings where she would present her ideas and thoughts. She spoke to her friends and families about her concerns and they reassured her that she would do fine. They gave her suggestions such as "Imagine everyone in their underwear" or "Keep practicing and it will get easier."

Feeling frustrated and worried about how this fear might impact her career, Molly decided to ask for help from the spiritual realm. After applying the phases taught in Chapters 4–6 (increasing vibration, releasing fears, and harmonizing through rituals), she said the words, *Spirit guides, I give you permission and accept your assistance for helping me through my fears of public speaking, and I thank you.* She said this daily in the shower while closing her eyes. She repeated the words slowly so that she could concentrate on receiving the energy of support around her. Saying this statement to herself made her realize she held a belief that people judged her. She gave herself permission to release the belief that she was not smart or capable. This awareness seemed to come out of nowhere. She knew it must have been brought to her intuitively. She acknowledged this by saying, *Thank you, spirit.* Her heart felt more open and less guarded. The next time she went to the meeting, she felt a resiliency emanating out from her. To her surprise, the symptoms toned down significantly.

Resiliency Helps You Enjoy Clarity

The gift of resiliency will bring you clarity in your approach to life. Clarity is freedom from ambiguity. It is becoming one with all that is happening, rather than dissecting each small part of your life. Your observations and awareness lead you to appreciate the bigger picture. Some, like poets, songwriters, or speakers, choose to describe this picture in words. Others choose to express and experience it silently, through art, or through other forms of creative expressions.

Clarity comes from understanding the value of your emotions, what they are, how they work, and the way they can be transformed into pure consciousness. It is the ability to distinguish a truth from an untruth, and the knowledge that lies show up in the subconscious and must be cleared. This awareness offers you a taste of the true power that you have. You can transform all beliefs and fears into higher vibrations. As a result, you no longer have the desire to hold back or suppress your emotions and beliefs.

When you are clear, your words, intentions, and actions unify as a consistent flow of energy. This flow is your gift of resiliency.

Once you receive it, it will no longer come and go. It is not dependent upon rewards, nor is it depleted by rejection. It is no longer something you pray for or worry about. Remember, you are already complete. You have this clarity inside you now. It is always available to you.

Speaking Soul

Anxiety gives you the impression that nothing you do works, everything you try fails, you are not enough, or you should do something more. Learning "soul talk" helps you transform these messages into the gift of resiliency. Despite the negative associations with it, anxiety does not want you to fail; it wants you to thrive. It is attempting to direct you to your soul. You cannot connect from lies. It is like trying to place a phone call when you have barely any service. The energy is low, dense, and weak. You have not failed; your soul heard the message and responded accordingly. With skill, awareness, and clarity this begins to change.

Just like when you ask the spiritual realm for help, "soul talk" requires the present tense. For example,

Instead of Saying . . .	Say . . .
I try	I am, I choose
I can't	I look forward to
I should	I know

Framing statements and intentions in that type of language connects them to the here and now, where your soul lives. The soul also speaks in pictures. When you see a picture or image that makes an impression on you or that you can feel in your heart, that's your soul speaking to you. Look around for images (sunrise, nature, animals) that strike your heart and the vibration of this will alter the way you see the situation. This, in turn, filters through the thoughts, words, and behaviors you choose that day.

Gift Tag

Skill: Soul Talk

The soul is the higher you. To speak to this part of yourself, use language that comes from the present moment. For example, rather than *I try*, state *I am*. Watch for lower-vibrational words such as *can't*, *won't*, and *should*, and replace them with words that allow the experience to come into the now, such as *have*, *experience*, and *know*. For example, *I have found additional ways to support my friend* or *I am willing to experience (rather than react to) a particular discomfort.*

CHAPTER 9

THE THIRD GIFT: HOPE

"We are products of our past, but we don't have to be prisoners of it."

—RICK WARREN, *THE PURPOSE DRIVEN LIFE*

Anxiety Focused: Feeling Fear

Gift Focused: Embrace Hope

Hope is the feeling inside you that lets you know something good is coming around the corner. You may not yet see it; however, you know it is there. Hope is being able to see your present circumstances as part of the progression toward your gifts. For many, it motivates you to keep going, try harder, and dig deeper. The gift of hope goes far beyond your drive and willpower. It is a feeling that provides a flow of energy permeated by courage. You'll need that courage to recognize and experience any vulnerability that shows up along your journey, in the form of your:

- Identity
- Thoughts
- Beliefs
- Attachments
- Attitudes
- Preconceived notions
- Expectations
- Fears

Courage will also help you surrender to what is keeping you afloat. Similar to the change in tides, it propels you in a new direction.

Hope can be learned or witnessed, directly as well as indirectly, perhaps through an inspiring story or a simple act of kindness. Transforming anxious feelings into conscious states also transforms hopeless states of fear and worry into love and faith. The process includes exploring what you are resisting. This chapter explores the gift of hope and the teachings behind it, the importance of optimizing your brain, honoring feelings, and releasing blockages, and the art of letting go.

Optimize Your Brain

Your brain, when nurtured and attended to, is like a well-oiled machine. The communication between your brain and your body runs clearly and efficiently. When necessary, the neurons in your brain and body:

- Fire off and circulate healthy doses of mood-boosting neurotransmitters such as dopamine and serotonin, which put systems such as your intestinal track and adrenal glands at ease.
- Reduce cortisol, one of the stress-induced hormones, so your overall view of the world changes. For example, when your adrenal glands are overworked and stress hormones dominate the brain and body, you may look in the mirror and only see your flaws. No matter how many times someone tells you how beautiful you are, your view is always the same. Without so much cortisol, you can see and appreciate yourself as you really are.

Creating a more hopeful view does require changing your thoughts. Your first priority, however, is to properly feed your body and brain. If your brain and body are malnourished, your quest to optimize your brain will be stymied. Your overall health puts in place the foundation for supporting the development of hope.

Fueling your body with exercise and nutrition make simple practices such as closing your eyes, breathing, eating, and moving mindfully seem like superpowers. Meditation and energy techniques take on a whole new meaning when your body is primed with hydration and whole foods. Similar to nurturing soil, the seeds are more likely to flourish from fertilized, watered ground. Think of the billions of neurons located in your brain as your seeds. Your thoughts and awareness determine how and where your neurons fire. Neurons that fire together wire together—meaning that by choosing to integrate self-care into your lifestyle, you are training your neurons to fire in a certain way. Over time, this alters your perception of how you view your world. Similar to updating programs on your computer, your brain is optimized to fit the lifestyle you have created. This lifestyle is likely to include emotions of gratitude, love, and hope.

Eat Healthy Foods

To begin, you will need to make sure you are eating foods that are rich in vitamins and minerals. This includes whole grains, dairy (or dairy substitute), vegetables, fruits, and protein sources (meats, fish, tofu, etc.). Healthy fats, such as the ones in nuts, avocado, coconut oil, and olive oil, are also essential. Working with a certified nutritionist or health counselor is something to consider if you struggle in this area. Often professionals such as these will suggest that you journal what you eat on a daily basis. They can objectively tell you how your brain and body may be deprived.

Hydration is equally important. Thirst is often the first sign of the body edging toward survival mode. Drinking purified water or noncaffeinated beverages will keep your body working efficiently for you.

Exercise

Exercise is another crucial component to optimizing your brain. A blend of cardio and strength training opens the doorway to seeing things in a new light. According to U.S. government recommendations, adults ages 18–64 should aim for at least two hours and thirty minutes of exercise per week (*www.health .gov*). This could include various types of exercise such as: biking, swimming, walking, running, dance, etc. According to the Anxiety and Depression Association of America, even as little as five minutes of aerobic exercise can begin to stimulate antianxiety effects—so every little bit counts! This mindset is especially important when you're trying to fit exercise into a busy lifestyle. Jim's situation is well known to many: He worked long hours operating a grocery store he owned, which left little time to exercise. He rarely sat down for meals, instead eating on the go, grabbing food while he worked or going for long periods of time without eating and then eating large amounts late at night. A recent visit to his doctor left him feeling frustrated and hopeless about his future. Not only was he overweight, but his cholesterol levels were alarmingly high. In addition to being placed on medication, Jim was advised to incorporate changes in his lifestyle.

Before meeting with a nutritionist, Jim was quite cynical. He covered up his feelings through sarcasm and joking around. He resisted making lifestyle changes, as he insisted things would fall apart at work without him. He justified his fears through countless examples of the things that had gone wrong when he was not present.

The nutritionist showed Jim how his on-the-go lifestyle was depleting his brain and body. Neurons were firing in support of maintaining his stressful views, rather than paving new neuropathways to others. She suggested that Jim start making changes to his lifestyle slowly. Since he was not exercising at all, she suggested he start by exercising two to three times per week for thirty minutes. She also made a few changes to his overall meal plan and taught him how to eat mindfully. She taught him skills such as eating earlier in the day (without distractions like the TV or computer), chewing more slowly, noticing the taste and smell of his food, and observing his surroundings without judgment. Using these skills, she encouraged him to try to sit down for at least one of the meals per day. Over the course of six weeks, Jim noticed not only a decrease in stress but an increase in energy. He lost several pounds and was amazed at how sitting and mindfully eating for just one meal a day grounded him. He found himself more upbeat and hopeful about the future.

Honor Your Feelings

In the earlier chapters, you learned how to purify your emotions by allowing yourself to experience them from beginning to middle to end. You also learned how to harmonize them through the development of rituals in your day. Respecting, accepting, and honoring the energy of your emotions as they are gives you the ability to actually feel any hopelessness you encounter and process that emotion. This process will help you find the gift of hope.

When things are heading in the "right" direction, you may more easily feel hopeful. Perhaps you receive a compliment or are able to see the results of your hard work—you pick up your paycheck or your child gives you a hug. When life does not give you a pat on the back, either monetarily or through tangible acknowledgments, the days may run together without any significance. Routines and tasks shape your moods rather than experiences. Taking time to honor your feelings helps you to purge what you are truly fearing, perhaps the loss of love, pride, connection, respect, or a sense of belonging.

To honor your feelings means to accept the energy in its raw form. Next time you brush your teeth, do it while watching a clock. Brush them for about ninety seconds. This will give you an idea of how long it takes to complete a feeling.

The emotion of hopelessness may feel like a weight pulling you down. Hopelessness blocks your viewpoint, similar to how it would feel to sit behind a tall person in a movie theater. Hopeless people tend to see themselves as victims or as having very little control over their circumstances. Rather than experiencing their discomfort, they become frustrated with it by finding ways to blame others. As a result, they may revert to anxiety, hate, anger, or regret. These emotions do have more movement, and therefore when expelled give you a release—but a temporary one. This release not only distracts you from hopelessness, but also gives you a shot of adrenaline. In the moment, the urge to tell someone off, quit school, break up with someone, or eat unhealthy food is more attractive than the observation of your feelings. This type of release is temporary and is often accompanied by consequences from your actions.

Transforming hopeless states into hopeful ones can only truly occur through love. As you apply the phases listed in Chapters 4–6 into your life, you'll lift your energy and stimulate vibrations of love. In these higher vibrations, you will imagine embracing the energy of hopelessness in your arms and giving it a hug. The following Gift Tag and sections will show you how to do that.

Gift Tag

Exercise: Hug Your Solar Plexus

Transforming states of hopelessness into states of hope requires you to place your attention on your body. Heavier energy often becomes congested in the pelvic area and the pit of your abdomen (below your navel). Either standing up or sitting down (without slouching), close your eyes, and place your hands on your abdomen. (Doing this exercise outside or as you gaze out a window can work really well.) Holding your abdomen, take three deep inhales and exhales. Your hands are very powerful and designed for self-healing. After three breaths, picture in your mind an image of hope, perhaps a rainbow, peace sign, apple tree, dove, clear sky, or sunrise. Nurture hopelessness by infusing the energy of this image into your body. You may find yourself wanting to extract hopelessness before infusing hope. This undermines the power of love. Love does all the work; there is no need for you to feel like you have to move something "bad" before stimulating the good. Trust the power of hope.

Letting Go of Being the Same

You are not meant to stay the same—physically or spiritually. Physically, you move through many developmental stages across your lifespan. Certainly, you can influence these stages by what you choose to focus on, practice, and emphasize in your life. A well-developed brain requires exercise through a variety of activities that strengthen your memory, motor coordination, and attention. Tasks such as reading, writing, crossword puzzles, socializing, exercise, and large and fine motor tasks, such as knitting, puzzles, and resistance training, assist with this. In addition, without realizing it, you are literally changing moment to moment, day to day. The millions of cells in your brain and body are constantly moving, connecting, and regenerating themselves. Your stomach lining, for example, replaces its cells every four days. Similar to a snake shedding its skin, your body is in a constant state of renewal.

You are also designed for spiritual change and growth. Your capability to *feel* not only gives you the adequacy to form deep, meaningful relationships but also activates your intuition and higher consciousness. You can connect with parts of yourself that go far beyond the scope of your conscious mind. Within these parts are additional forms of insight and guidance. For many, the word *spiritual* may be associated with a specific religion or characterized by a life without possessions or a hippie, free-floating attitude. Spirituality doesn't have to mean that, however. Your spiritual self is simply the part of you that is willing to ask, *Who am I?* or *How may I serve today?* knowing that your insight will change and grow as you encounter the emotional, at times painful, experiences that life brings. It is what you choose to do with the knowledge you receive that strengthens this part of who you are.

Release Attachments That Are Holding You Back

States of hopelessness reveal what you are attached to. Following are some common attachments found in the human experience. Things or attachments are not the problem; it is the fear of losing them. This triggers controlling, at times neurotic behavior, which restrains you from experiencing flow.

Attachments	Reactions
Thoughts	Possessive
Expectations	Agendas
Distractibility	Fear, control

The gift of hope leads you to the energy of grace. Grace is the deep part of you that knows none of what you see and have is all yours. Your children, family, and community members also belong to the universe. Each person arrives with a plan. Some may call it God's plan, but regardless of the terminology you use, you are part of it. Rest assured, all plans are meant to come with change.

To let go means to believe in something greater. It gives you the ability to not only feel hopeful but also to be hopeful. Being hopeful and telling yourself to be hopeful may have different energies. For example, you may say out loud, *I hope for the best*, but subconsciously you are preparing for the worst. The symptoms of anxiety remind you of who you are not. The process of letting go includes opening your mind, body, and heart to something more. Instead of embracing the 10 percent of your conscious mind as the primary resource for approaching your life, you can choose to allow the emergence of other parts of yourself. This includes your intuition, subconscious, and spiritual connection. Letting go is when you say, *I am more than this* and *I trust my higher self will guide me through.*

Your attachments to fear and doubt can breed hopelessness. For example, Billy worked for the same company for seven years. He was successful, but for years he had experienced a feeling that he was being held back from something more. When these feelings started to arise inside him, he would distract himself or talk himself out of them. He would tell himself, *You have a good job, it pays well, and after all you have a family to support. To go off on your own would be selfish and risky.* Although Bill felt hopeful about his future, a small part of him also felt hopeless. After all, he had spent years working on his education and career, and he secretly feared that he made the wrong choice.

One day, Bill was unexpectedly laid off. Caught off-guard, he felt angry, betrayed, and unappreciated for his years of loyalty. He was embarrassed, ashamed, and worried about his reputation. After allowing himself to feel his deep shame and admitting to his wife and close friends some of his deepest fears, Billy mustered enough courage to go out on his own. Individually, he prayed and asked for guidance. Instead of asking for his prayers to help him, he prayed for the strength to let go and forgive. The courage and hope he received not only led him to start his own business, but he also found himself earning more money and enjoying more personal freedom than before.

Continually Let Go
You may currently associate letting go with fixing or getting rid of thoughts, beliefs, situations, and experiences that do not serve

you. This may very well be the outcome from your intentions. But keep in mind that letting go also means to have faith and trust in your own vibrations. Letting go is not an occasional act but rather a daily practice of releasing lower vibrations and raising higher ones.

Hope states are increased by your ability to visualize. Imagine placing fear in the palm of your hand, and notice how it feels, perhaps cold, shaky, and heavy. Just imagine yourself as big as the sun, shining your light on this fear and sending it warm, melting sensations. Engage your breath while doing so. The following Gift Tag offers a guided meditation for letting go.

Gift Tag

Meditation: Letting Go

Find a quiet place and either sit up straight or lie down. Close your eyes and breathe in and out of your nose a few times. Relax the muscles in your face, your eyebrows, shoulders, arms, torso, legs, feet, and so on. Mentally trace your skin, internal organs, and bloodstream with each breath. Allow your body to be heavy and relaxed.

After a few minutes, keeping your eyes closed and continuing to relax your body, begin to bring into your mind any thoughts, beliefs, hardships, emotions, expectations, or experiences you would like to let go of today. It could also be a role or identity that you have assumed that does not represent your purpose. Perhaps you have taken on the identity of a strong person who never needs love and affection, or the role of taking care of others before attending to your own needs. Maybe you have pretended to believe or behave in ways that aren't really a part of who you are. Choose one or two things that come to mind and trust that those are the ones you are ready to let go of today.

Once selected, notice the areas of your body that feel tight or constricted when you bring these images or thoughts into your mind. Perhaps your abdomen, chest, neck, or lower back feel knotted. As you recognize these areas, pay attention to any resistance or ambivalence you may experience. For example, you may find yourself wanting to open your eyes to take yourself out of the experience. If you do, give yourself permission to close your eyes and relax once again for a little bit longer. As you notice these areas, picture a loving, peaceful image in your mind. It may be an image of nature (sun, moon, water, mountains) or a heartfelt memory of special people. Allow these higher vibrations to dissolve the energy that has sustained the thoughts and beliefs you have chosen today. Take a few more breaths and then place what it is you are choosing to let go inside a balloon and imagine yourself letting it go.

Release What Is Blocking You

Hope gives you the courage to see beyond lack or fear. By releasing what is blocking you, you are able to make a clear distinction between hopeful energy and situations that offer the illusion of hope. This skill will be of great service to you as it strengthens your ability to see clearly what is hindering you.

Keep in mind, blocks are not about what is bad or good. They are simply forms of resistance. Some resistance can actually be guidance. For example, you may feel yourself being ambivalent about going to a party or making an important decision. This may in fact be for your greater good because it points out to you that you should take some time to process your feelings about the situation. Blocks can also be a way that you hold illusions in place. Illusions are developed by beliefs that promote you as being separate from spirit. Your spirit is endless and infinite, yet you might experience beliefs that impose strict borders or limitations that are upheld by subconscious blocks. The tools in Chapters 4–6 give you everything you need to release them. As always, it is important for you to listen to what you feel instead of attempting to figure it out or understand it. Attempting to understand something can easily lead to judgment. Nothing can grow or be released in judgment.

To truly grasp the gift of hope, it is important for you to release any resistance you have to feeling fear. As human beings, our brains have been conditioned to survive. Feeling fear has been biochemically imprinted into your brain as a means of warning you about threats to your safety. Your body may actually be equating fear with death on some level. The only way to move through this fear is to make a conscious connection to love. Love triumphs over fear, always.

Picture a brick wall. The bricks represent your emotions, and the cement in between the bricks is your resistance. In order to experience the emotion, you must first move through the cement (resistance). Rather than imagining yourself smashing through the wall, see the wall dissolving as you break down the cement holding it together. The gift of hope sits within that space. Here's an example of someone who encountered her brick wall: Joanne had experienced anxiety her entire life, in school, social groups, and occasionally at work. One of the ways she taught herself to cope was by maintaining a clean, well-organized environment. In her home, work space, and even her car, she spent a considerable amount of time cleaning and shifting things around. When Joanne's belongings were out of place or messy, she felt uneasy and easily frustrated. She made straightening things up her priority, leaving little time for her to relax and be present. Through spiritual counseling, Joanne realized she had a deep resistance to feeling fear. She held these feelings at bay by keeping herself busy and attempting to control how things appeared around her.

In order to support Joanne through her resistance, I taught her how to increase her vibrations of love. Through deep breathing (see Chapter 4) and guided visualizations, Joanne learned how to strengthen her energy inside and out. I encouraged Joanne to picture herself blowing bubbles on a beautiful day. I asked her to imagine placing her resistance to feel inside the bubbles, then to watch the bubbles float around and allow them to pop. I then had her give her resistance a color or image. She chose a dark, heavy blob of energy. Next, I asked her to put this image inside the bubble and again watch it pop. She did and described seeing gooey black liquid come out of the bubble. Next, I asked her to imagine herself in a large, clear bubble. Through breathing work and tuning in to the sensations on her skin and scalp, I had her imagine the bubble getting larger and larger, to the point where it extended far beyond her body. After a few minutes of allowing this bubble to grow, I reminded her that feeling and sensing your energy is no different from feeling and sensing love. If you feel soothed, lifted, and expanded in your awareness, you are in a state of love. Love is limitless. Once she was able to make this connection, Joanne allowed the imaginary bubble around her to pop. She did this not because she knew it was the right thing, but rather because she could feel the strength of her own love, and how capable of overcoming fear (resistance) it was.

When you meet energy blockages in the body with fear, it is similar to hitting that brick wall. This may lead you down a narrow path of limited alternatives. You may even hear yourself say, *I don't have a choice.* In those cases, in essence you are giving fear the upper hand. The reality is fear is only as real as you make it. Fear is not capable of growth and expansion; love is. If you access the gift of hope, love will take the place of the resistance you feel. Your gift of hope can bring you a whole different view of your life and its limitless possibilities.

Gift Tag

Reflection: Detect Hopeful Energy

Hopeful energy reflects your wholeness, as opposed to what you lack. Be mindful of advertisements and solicitations that imply you are "less than," such as fad diets or makeup promises. Notice the times you are drawn to something or someone. Is it their energy or their promise to make you whole? Be open and willing to receive the gifts that are offered around you. If you feel a sense of love, honesty, authenticity, and compassion, it is likely you are detecting hope. Notice if people open up to you as well. This, too, is a sign that you are giving off hopeful vibrations. If their openness uplifts you, take it as a compliment. If you feel drained by situations or people, it may be an illusion of hope—in that case, you may want to respectfully set a boundary so you are not affected by it.

CHAPTER 10

THE FOURTH GIFT: EMPATHY

---

*"I think we all have empathy.
We may not have enough courage
to display it."*

—MAYA ANGELOU

Anxiety Focused: Being Judgmental

Gift Focused: Feeling Empathy

Empathy, the ability to feel the emotions of others, to be able to put yourself in their shoes, is hardwired into the human brain. Empathy offers you an internal experience of what others are feeling. According to Dr. Helen Riess, associate clinical professor of psychiatry at Harvard Medical School, it gives you the ability to see the specialness in someone else. Likewise, others can reflect your specialness back to you.

Anxiety, when misunderstood and feared, distorts your view of empathy. As a result you may find yourself taking things personally or develop worrisome responses or a victim mentality. This not only weakens your energy but negates your good intentions. When received as a gift, empathy allows you to relate to another's experience from higher-vibrational states rather than by becoming a vibrational match to the situation. Just because you can relate to someone's experience does not mean you need to travel down the road of losing energy as a way to display your hurt or concern. The gift of empathy is being able to be there for someone else through the absorption of the energy of your own love.

This chapter teaches about the connection between empathy and your soul. It begins with widening your comprehension of empathy so you understand how it works for you and the person you are relating to. Since it's a bridge to your soul, empathy is a great reminder of your purpose. As your gift, it reveals parts of you and capabilities that you may not have developed yet, such as:

- Your authenticity
- Your ability to forgive
- Your emotional flow

- The ability to remove unnecessary competition
- The courage to address painful situations

Empathy as Personal Growth

Empathy differs from sympathy. *Sympathy* means to express genuine sorrow and concern for another, while *empathy* allows you to relate on a more personal level. For example, you may empathize with another mother of a toddler having a tantrum because you have been in her shoes. Or perhaps you are less judgmental toward someone who is an alcoholic because you too have been there. Your personal connection is far more powerful than sympathy. Take a moment and put yourself in someone else's shoes. If you were having a problem with your relationship would you gravitate toward someone who sympathizes with you or someone who can empathize with you? People often choose people who have been in their situation.

Empathy opens your heart, strengthening your ability to listen and be compassionate. People sense your heart vibrations and may be naturally drawn to you. This does not mean you have to stop everything you are doing and help everyone that comes your way. Take it as a compliment that you have this ability, and focus on quality versus quantity. Know that person's situation is being presented to you for more than one reason, such as:

1. So you can offer your empathy and compassion
2. To elicit the release of certain vibrations in you

Empathy has its own way of revealing your fears, judgments, beliefs, and lower-vibrating emotions. People and circumstances are often a reflection of unfinished emotions and self-limiting beliefs. For example, your partner's sense of unworthiness may trigger the unworthiness that exists in you. It is through our relationships that we discover the areas we have not yet fully developed. Emotions such as jealousy and envy stem from insecurity and, when left unexplored, sit like poison in the body. This contaminates your thoughts and vibrations, as well as those of the individuals around you. If you feel jealous of someone else, ask your higher self to help you clear it. Make a conscious choice to no longer carry that emotion in your body. Take deep breaths and visualize it lifting from your body like steam. Acknowledging and clearing low-vibrating emotions lifts your empathic vibrations. As this occurs, you are able to make a powerful shift from *I relate to your suffering* or *I become your suffering* to *I honor the significance of your emotional pain.*

Feeling Others' Pain Without Absorbing It

It's not easy to allow yourself to feel the pain of others without taking it on as your own. As you develop this skill, not only will you be able to relate to and support others without sacrificing your own energy, but you will also be able to identify and let your emotions come to fruition.

Chapter 11 gives you more information on how to support and share your gifts with others. For now, it is important that you take in and receive this gift of empathy. You may have been conditioned to skip over yourself and immediately give to others. If you do, you will only find yourself feeling frustrated later. Your efforts will appear to fall short. The following list may help you identify the differences. They are subtle, but they're important. Keep in mind, you can be both sympathetic and empathetic at the same time.

Sympathy	The Gift of Empathy
Care and concern for others	Feeling what others feel, because you have been there
Recognition of someone's suffering	Standing by someone who is feeling pain while generating the vibration of your own love
Compassion for others	Trusting and believing your higher vibrations create compassion in you

Empathy Helps You Relate to Your Soul

As you develop your awareness of yourself, empathy evolves into something more than simply relating to another person's feelings or circumstances. It is also a way to relate to the soul of another, and through that experience you get to know the strength of your own spirit. Ultimately empathy allows you to relate to your own soul—the part of you that yearns to grow, contribute, make a difference, and support others. This gift is strengthened by your breath, reviewing your progress regularly, and cutting the ties from all things that suck your life force.

When you hear someone say, *Everything happens for a reason*, they are pondering on their soul. For some, the soul speaks quickly, offering bright ideas in short spurts; for others, it speaks through dreams and visions. Your soul knows you have the ability to empathize even if you have disconnected or have never been permitted to fortify this ability. Consider some of the events and emotional circumstances you have encountered to be your soul's attempt to develop this in you, or for you to be a way to develop it in others.

Anxiety and its symptoms, when misunderstood and fought against, may tug you toward becoming self-absorbed. You may find yourself needing attention, complaining, breaking down easily, avoiding certain situations, or resisting change. In the book *Soul Centered*, author Sarah McLean employs the term *soul-centered* to describe "a particular shift in perspective," explaining: "When you're soul-centered, you are not dependent on others for your sense of self or worthiness. Instead, you are guided by an inner reference point—your own soul."

Your soul could never be captured in words alone. Its resiliency, possibility, and power are impossible to measure. However, there are a couple of things each soul is interested in:

1. Your growth
2. How you influence others along the way

Imagine standing on a mountaintop after a long, arduous climb. Your soul wants you to make that climb, withstand the trials and tribulations, notice the temptations, and be able to stand in your truth and worthiness. It also wants you to reach out to others and give them a lift along the way. This is not to be confused with carrying or rescuing them. To rescue means to take on the perceived problems and solutions of another as if they were your own. You may actually do things for them—that's misusing empathy. For example, empathy is misused when you take it upon yourself to interrupt or remove the emotional pain of another. This gives the impression that pain is not only wrong for that person, but too frightening for him to experience. It is a way of meeting pain with fear rather than holding it through love. When you notice the empathetic feelings that run through your body while breathing in love and compassion, you empower others to face their pain on their own.

Keeping Empathy as You Grow

Your soul wants you to grow. In order to do this, it is essential that you take time to reflect on your progress. When you are in a perpetual forward motion, it's important to take a moment to pause and celebrate how far you have come. By doing so, you strengthen empathy. Not only do you get to identify with the trials and tribulations of another, but you are also able to relate to the climb. You see the path of progress in yourself and in others. Anxiety, when viewed as a problem, puts you on the track of wanting things to be different. It notices weaknesses before growth and overfocuses on outcome instead of progress. Parents in particular can identify with this type of anxiety, as the rush of daily life can lead you to zoom into what is wrong rather than what is right. For example, Alison was a mother of three boys. She worked part-time so that she could be home when her children arrived from school. Although she was grateful for her part-time hours, she often felt frustrated and easily annoyed with her boys' behavior. Bedtime was particularly stressful. She had to give several reminders and found the process to be long and exhausting. One of her boys was sensitive and rarely spoke about his worries until it was time to go to bed. It seemed that just when she was about to kiss him good night, he would want to share something about his day. Being exhausted herself, she tried to rush the experience, telling him it would be fine and to go to bed. Although this seemed to work in the moment, she often found later that she would feel guilty for not being more empathetic.

Empathy becomes shortsighted when it is seen as something to do or a way to fulfill a role. Your gift of empathy goes far beyond what you can do for others, however. It is a way to console and replenish your own fears and anxieties with love. It is the part of you that says, *Who I am matters* and *My awareness is enough*. Receiving the gift of empathy is no different from receiving the energy of compassion. It is a vibration that runs through you and extends outward to anyone you come in contact with. When empathy becomes weakened, you have probably learned to attach certain images and expectations to it. You're rejecting empathy when you review your day from a standpoint of what you did wrong or how things should have gone. Like a CD that automatically gets pushed out of a player, stating that it is unreadable, empathy is ejected rather than instilled and played from the heart.

You know this has occurred when you wake up or move about your day expecting what will happen. Alison eventually realized that she was expecting bedtime to be a problem. It is likely that her body had a memory of being triggered both psychologically and physiologically at bedtime. Anxiety not only loves but thrives off predictability. The soul, on the other hand, resonates with the flow and vibration of your own energy rise.

To help Alison connect to her soul, it was important for her to develop ways to release her expectations—particularly the ones that fed her sense of failure and unworthiness. She was able to do so by developing a ritual she could use at the beginning or end of the day. For her, it was sitting in the same chair that looked out a window where she could see the trees and sky while taking three deep breaths. On inhale, she closed her eyes and visualized spaciousness (such as a beach or the ocean) and on exhale, she imagined herself picking up sand, squeezing it in the palm of her hand, and then slowly letting it slip through, releasing it back down to the ground. On days she felt really tense, she would even squeeze her palms into fists as she did this.

Additional ways to release the day are on inhale to float your arms up in the air, stating a mantra such as *I choose to renew or refresh this day* and on exhale bring them down. Pretending to cut the ties from people, things, beliefs, and thoughts that drain you can also be very effective. Ties are like a loose piece of string hanging from your clothes. You could go months without seeing it. When you get scissors and cut off the string, your shirt may appear less tattered or worn. Expectations are similar, only instead, they are invisible energetic attachments that pull and hang from you. Through your imagination you can visualize cutting them off as you end or start the day.

Gift Tag

Reflection: Review Your Progress

Take a moment and ponder all the progress you have made in the last week, month, or even year. Try not to put a weight or value on each success. Allow even the simple victories to emerge, such as: *I am taking time to breathe, read more, notice the good, soften my expectations, go outside,* or *watch my thoughts.*

Living a Nonjudgmental Life

This section takes your gift of empathy one step further. Empathy helps you relate to your soul and to others, but it is also highly linked to you being worthy of acceptance. To truly empathize with another, it must come from a place of nonjudgment. This may be difficult to swallow, as anxiety is often sustained through judgments about yourself and others. Judgments not only increase the pressure of anxiety symptoms, but also keep them alive—thus never really allowing them to transform into something greater.

To approach someone or something with nonjudgment is a way to approach it from your whole self, which includes you as a self-healer. This may seem impossible to you, as your anxiety prompts you to pick things apart and analyze. Judgment is when you evaluate something or someone with the mindset that some things are good and others are bad. Of course, using your better judgment is essential in certain situations. Not only does it keep you safe, but it also helps you make sound choices that are for your highest good as well as the good of others. This type of judgment is not what this section is referring to. It is referring to judgment of your emotions and the experiences they relate to. When you judge your emotions, you deprive yourself of truly feeling them. The symptoms of anxiety are a reminder to you that there is more for you to feel. Depriving yourself of opportunities to feel contributes to the perception that you have no choice in the matter.

How to Avoid Unnecessary Judgment

Practicing nonjudgment has very little to do with *doing*, and everything to do with *being*. EFT, or tapping acupressure (discussed in Chapter 4), as a way to raise your vibration is a very effective way to process emotions in a nonjudgmental way. Part of the reason it is successful is because the energy of the emotions is brought up lovingly. For example, while tapping the side of your hand (halfway between the base of the pinkie and wrist) you might say, *Even though I am feeling nervous, I completely and totally love myself.* Another example would be, *Even though I am feeling judgmental, I completely and totally love myself.*

Judgment typically shows up as pressure or blame, or through a preoccupation with someone or something. When you judge your own emotions, you are denying the development and power of your intuition. You may automatically distrust or question your feelings rather than accept them as they are. Judgment holds your feelings hostage, therefore depriving you of your gifts. Acceptance, on the other hand, gives you the courage to move through emotions you may have never imagined moving through.

Judgment can affect your physical body as well as your emotions. On the outside, Laura appeared quiet and reserved. She was hard working, yet also made an attempt to bring balance into her life through diet and exercise. This did seem to decrease her stress; however, inwardly she had a difficult time exploring and sharing her feelings. One day, while taking a yoga class Laura kept falling over in the balancing postures. Although she felt inwardly frustrated, on the outside she hid it by keeping a smile on her face. Her yoga teacher (who was also a psychologist) suggested that sometimes when you fall out of a posture it may be due to heaviness in your heart. Similar to a scale, if more weight is distributed to one side, the scale will tip in that direction.

The teacher suggested she focus on the heaviness in her heart with nonjudgment. To initiate this process, she had Laura go through all the possible feelings in her heart using EFT (tapping). After about one minute of tapping Laura could physically feel the energy in her heart move into her throat and then eventually dissipate completely. As the heaviness dissipated she felt her gaze soften and lips loosen as she regained her balance. Not only could she balance better, but when she did fall out of a posture she was able to put herself back in it with nonjudgment and ease. It no longer mattered to her whether or not she fell. What mattered was the experience of her own energy and her ability to touch base with her authentic self, who did not judge her.

Gift Tag

Skill: Intuitive Breathing

Research has shown that taking long, deep breaths that stem from the lower abdomen and exaggerate the exhale may alleviate symptoms of anxiety. Blocking off the right nostril and breathing exclusively through the left (inhaling and exhaling) a few times is also effective (described in Chapter 4). The aim for all of the techniques offered to you in this book is to get you in touch with your intuitive breath. That means following the type of breathing that feels right to you at that moment. If exhaling feels right, trust and go with that breath. If you feel the urge to inhale deeply, then allow the fullness of that breath to emerge. The idea is that one day, you will begin to move and breathe in your body intuitively with nonjudgment.

Practice Love Through Forgiveness

When you choose to move through emotions such as bitterness, resentment, hurt, and revenge, you find forgiveness on the other side. No doubt, you'll encounter situations when forgiveness seems impossible—for example, when there is harm done to innocent people, children, and animals. Empathy at that point seems like a far reach from being able to relate on a personal level. Imagining yourself in the shoes of a mother, wife, husband, father, sister, or brother may come easily . . . but how can you possibly relate to some of the evil acts that occur in the world? Some acts of violence are beyond comprehension and in many cases it will be your faith in something greater that pulls you through. Meditations and prayers that call on higher-vibrational assistance are the way humans can work together consciously to create more love in the world. Rather than armor up through nonforgiveness, consider strengthening one of the most powerful forces known to man—love. Supporting the flow of your emotions while calling on vibrational assistance is a powerful way to achieve this.

Forgiveness is an act of courage and a testament to faith. Bringing this idea into your mind may bring up a burial ground of emotions, one being the uncertainty that life can bring. Receiving the gift of empathy is not solely about the possibility of forgiving others, but also a way to forgive yourself. As you do, you reach the underbelly of anxiety. When the symptoms of anxiety reoccur (even after you have committed to and applied techniques such as the ones in this book), it may be your soul's way of reminding you that you have not yet fully forgiven yourself. To truly forgive yourself, you must be willing to ask yourself the following questions.

Have I forgiven myself for . . .

1. Expecting more from others than they are ready and able to give?
2. Taking on traits that are toxic toward others?
3. Behaving in ways that do not serve others and me?
4. All the times I believed I was less than, incapable, or unworthy?
5. Disrespecting or disregarding my growth and journey?

Forgiveness is rarely taught directly. You have witnessed it or been exposed to it through books, news stories, or religion. Often it is described as a spiritual experience, a way to awaken to the realization that each and every human being on the planet is a soul experiencing a journey. Attempting to understand forgiveness from the human part of self, the part that wants to know how and why, may pose a challenge. As you learn to approach the spiritual realm with trust, this will decrease and the connection to your life events as part of a larger plan will get clearer.

Receiving the gift of empathy helps you to reflect on your life in a new way. Like getting a new pair of glasses, you are able to see the significance of your journey. This includes objective views of your world as a young child, preadolescent, adolescent, young adult, adult, and older adult. Your viewpoint takes in many different angles, perhaps as a sibling, neighbor, friend, coworker, teacher, colleague, roommate, spouse, and more. Viewing your life in this way opens the doorway to forgiveness. To cultivate an attitude of forgiveness it is important to recognize your personal evolution. Be willing to take inventory of the different phases and stages of your life with nonjudgment. Take a moment and see your history through the eyes of your inner child, open your heart, and allow the vulnerability of forgiveness to rise closer to the surface.

Gift Tag

Exercise: Attitude of Forgiveness

Picture a box full of old pictures of yourself. Each picture holds an experience or story, and each is connected to a wealth of emotions. As you sort through the box, notice the energy in the container as well as in your body. Do you feel nervous, scared, ambivalent, excited, joyful, or ashamed? Sorting through this box is a way to take your emotional inventory of those feelings that have been left untouched, ignored, held in, or pushed away. Allow the energy of the pictures to brush against your hands. Pick up each one similar to how you might weed a garden. Reach down deep and tug at the roots while noticing the texture, weight, and temperature of the weed in your hands. As you clear away old, congested energy, see yourself cultivating a space for an attitude of forgiveness. See this space as fertilized by your open energy and spiritual roots.

Empathy Brings Emotional Flow

Empathy offers you emotional flow. This is when your feelings flow freely through you, similar to a natural spring of water. Contrary to what you may believe, emotional flow is different from "being emotional." In emotional flow, you feel your feelings and those of others, without becoming overwhelmed or weighed down by them. You are then able to:

- Notice and feel your sensations through an observant state of mind
- Take in the vibrations of your emotions through your senses

- Hear your inner voice—the voice that guides you toward what feels right despite the way things may appear or what you have been told

Messages embedded in society are constantly challenging your ability to tune in to this flow. This is particularly true for the messages that state, repeat, and trigger vibrations of not being or having enough: money, education, good grades, patience, exercise, healthy choices, beauty, attention given to the ones you love and who love you, and the list goes on and on. Guess what? This same voice crumbles empathy. Emotional flow and being emotional speak different languages, as shown in this table.

Being Emotional	Emotional Flow
Reactive	Living in the present
Need to do or say something	Observing/listening
Consumed by thinking	Choosing feeling
Choosing to follow fear	Choosing to call on love

Using Empathy to Manage Emotions

Doug was the father of two teenage daughters. Although he loved his daughters very much, he often found himself at a loss for how to handle the emotional ups and downs that came along with adolescence and being a parent. When he felt tension or heard bickering in the room, the voice inside his head told him to either get away or tell them to stop. Although he felt bad about this, particularly because his wife was left carrying the burden of listening to his girls, the tension literally scared him away.

Doug never really pictured himself as being emotional until he learned how it was different from emotional flow. He learned how the tension caused by the girls bickering elicited unwanted memories and emotions from his childhood. Through counseling and guided meditation, Doug was able to notice and experience the sensations in his body. He was surprised to see how much the process of recognizing the sensations was able to soothe his mind and relax his body. The next time Doug was around tension in the home, he noticed how these sensations vacated his body, similar to what would occur if a real threat of danger were nearing him. Once he noticed this, he then gave himself permission to leave the room. Instead of distracting himself with work or projects, he took a minute to call the vibrations (sensations) back into his body. Think of how you might call your children or dog home for the night—only instead of using your voice and words, call them with your energy. By closing his eyes, taking deep breaths, and imagining his energy spreading from him like rings in a pond, he would tend to his children through his raised vibration. As Doug practiced this, he found that he was not only able to calm himself down in less than a minute but also increase his emotional flow. This strengthened his ability to re-enter the situation as a listener and also as a strong force of loving support as opposed to fear. To his surprise, the bickering decreased and he was more able to handle his daughters' behaviors authoritatively using a firm yet empathic approach.

Achieving Divine Wisdom

The term *divine wisdom* sounds like a vast realm of knowledge that only chosen ones, wise philosophers, or other "special" people have. On the contrary, divine wisdom lives in you and everyone else. You've had it all along—but accessing the gift of empathy helps bring you closer to seeing it in yourself. Divine wisdom is the energy that moves through you as you encounter states of emotional flow. It is your connection to higher vibrational realms where God, angels, saints, Buddha, life force, and other supreme life forces reside. Some people describe it as a moment when they feel held by the universe or when they feel the presence of something greater. It may be as subtle as the wind blowing on your face or a profound perceptual shift in the way you see the symptoms of anxiety. It could also be the energetic reconstruction of your life's story, an unveiling of your blessings, or the download of information that occurs unconsciously as you sit in meditation, prayer, or silence.

Divine wisdom is an inner knowing or belief that all your prayers, intentions, and requests have been heard, even if you have no direct proof or evidence. It reminds you that your life's journey is nonlinear, meaning what may appear to be a regression may be an opportunity for spiritual maturation. You might take two steps forward and one step back—but you're always making progress. Divine wisdom does not speak in pages but in chapters—it's easier to recognize when you look at the big picture. Very often, it is not until after the fact that you are able to look back and connect all the "dots"—the sequence of events and experiences that needed to take place in order for you to get where you are today.

Anxiety can support beliefs such as *No one understands me* or make you feel as if you are not able to be who you really are. Divine wisdom is listening and hearing your own point of view at all times. In other words, it is empathizing with yourself. Divine wisdom can provide you with experiences that will reflect what you are thinking and believing at all times. Consider the universe to be the ultimate empathizer—the universe is always hearing you. By choosing to lift your vibrations and consciously alter your thoughts while clearing your beliefs, the reflections around you will change.

Tapping into your divine wisdom is a way to build confidence and strength, and to expand your support system. The symptoms of anxiety magnify where your supports are lacking or have somehow failed you. Not only does this dim the ability to see and sense the abundance around you, but it also causes you to overfocus on what is limited. Divine wisdom is what you will receive when you allow yourself to communicate through higher vibrations by tuning in to the moment and incorporating practices that connect you to your higher beliefs. The beliefs you'll embrace see all beings as a source of love, despite what you may have been taught. The following Gift Tag offers you a meditation intended to connect you to the energy of grace. Feel free to improvise or make any changes that are more in line with the techniques you are comfortable with. Try it daily or more often as needed. The more often you do it, the stronger your connection to grace becomes.

Gift Tag

Meditation: Evoke Grace

Sit down comfortably in a chair with your spine upright. It may help you to sit near an open window so you can feel the breeze or sense the light on your face. Gently move your head back so it lines up with your body rather than jutting out in front of your shoulders. Allow yourself to take a deep breath. If your body wants to exhale first, then allow yourself to sink into the exhale by tugging your navel back. If your body chooses to inhale first, allow this by lifting your heart and chest up toward your chin to create more space. Close your eyes and relax your jaw by separating your back teeth.

You may notice as you breathe that your thoughts need a few moments to calm themselves down. Picture your thoughts like a distracted puppy or a small child that continues to be active before he falls asleep. Imagine petting the small puppy or rubbing the child's back as a way to calm him down. Do this with your breath. Each breath is a way to gently stroke the energy around your body. Picture taking a comb and brushing your energy down your body, beginning at the top of your head and brushing down to your toes. As you do this, imagine combing all the scattered energy around you back into your body where it can be experienced and transformed into higher vibrations.

Next, imagine a white light above your head shining down on you from the heavens. See this light penetrating your entire inner and outer body. If it feels comfortable, call on your spiritual support system—this may be God, Jesus, Buddha, universal life force, spiritual guides, masters, archangels, or another source—and ask them to surround and support you with the energy of grace. If not, simply call on the energy of grace through a silent intention. Either way, keep in mind, grace may show up as light, sensation, increased vibration, symbols, silence, images, sounds, or even words. Trust that your request has been heard and avoid placing a value or expectation on what you receive. Even if you feel blank or distracted, trust that your requests have been heard. Give yourself a moment to sit with the energy and if you like you may even choose to expand it as if you were blowing up a bubble. You may do this by inhaling and exhaling, picturing your body as a pillar of grace, and allowing it to emanate from you as it filters into your environment.

Surrendering Competition

Anxiety and its tendency to occupy low-vibrating emotions may bring about unnecessary competition and fear. Healthy competition is positive—it can be a way to motivate people to stick with a task, put forth more effort, and try to reach beyond their goals.

Unnecessary competition is different. It causes your energy to be depleted and consumed by insecurity. Opening yourself up to empathy changes how you view others. It does this by allowing you to notice others without fearing them. As a result, you become less preoccupied with or hung up on circumstances beyond your control. This focus pools your energy in higher vibrations, offering you clarity, insight, and guidance toward circumstances that align with your values and abundant nature.

As you create emotional flow, notice how you may be guided in a new direction. For example, you may find you no longer gravitate toward certain people. People and situations that once appeared to be in your best interest but are not become more transparent. What you once thought served you feels different. Your ability to sense alternative agendas, greed, and unnecessary competition is sharpened.

Unnecessary competition can happen with anyone and anywhere. It happens with neighbors, employees, businesses, schools, and professionals. Without awareness that it's happening, it sparks negativity and fear. It is an energy that puts you on alert when no immediate threat is present. You may even pick it up unconsciously through language. For example, the tone or quality of energy exerted when someone says "my client," "my customer," or "my school" is unnecessarily competitive. It is not so much the words or syntax, but rather the energy behind it. The reality is no one really owns anyone or anything. As human beings we do not own the planet; we are simply guests here carrying out a spiritual experience. By replacing the word *my* with *our*, you send out an energy of oneness and respect the service of others: for example, "our planet," "our customers," or "our community." Notice the difference between stating "my client" versus "a client." One of the most loving acts you can do is to give someone the freedom to choose. One person may come to you for a service, but in reality they always have the free will to leave. When you hold on to them energetically or assume they will stick with you, no matter what you are stifling their growth. Let them go and those who are meant to be part of your path will stick around. There is enough for everyone and when you release unnecessary competition it is likely the energy of abundance (rather than fear or lack) will return to you.

You know you are in emotional flow when you err on the side of staying true to who you are. Culturally you may have been conditioned to believe someone's status or accomplishments are reflections of who they are. As you access the gift of empathy, this too changes. Instead of sizing up others or making assumptions about their character, you become a spectator of their soul. Upholding this position allows you to reserve the space for others to live their purpose, become resilient, embrace hope, and feel empathy.

In South Africa the word *Sawubona* is a Zulu greeting that means "I see you." According to Bridget Edwards the response to *Sawubona* is *Ngikhona*, which means "I am here." The word *namaste*, used often in yoga, means "the light in me sees the light in you" or "the God in me sees the God in you." The gift of empathy takes you beyond hello and goodbye, allowing you a communion of spirit with those around you. This increases your capacity to recognize and release anxious thoughts, beliefs, and behaviors that no longer serve you. As a result, the energy that you once experienced as anxiety transforms into what comforts, soothes, and offers you peace of mind.

Gift Tag

Exercise: Releasing an Addiction to Thinking
If thinking gets in the way of your ability to empathize with yourself and others, it will be important for you to recognize this and give yourself permission to clear it. First, if this resonates with you, identify it by saying, *I notice.* For example, *I notice I am having a lot*

of thoughts, or *I notice the tension in my head and neck*. Next, say out loud to yourself, *I choose to clear and release any addiction to thinking*. Close your eyes and take deep breaths while relaxing your body. You can do this standing up or sitting upright in a chair. Visualize your thoughts as liquid light pouring down your head, neck, spine, lower back, legs, and feet. Relax your jaw, neck, and shoulders. Keep breathing, allowing your belly to expand on inhale and your navel to draw in on exhale. Imagine your addiction (not your thoughts) dissolving, similar to an ice cube melting in the sun.

CHAPTER 11

SHARING YOUR GIFTS

"Service through stuff is easy because it doesn't touch your world and it makes you feel good. Service through empowerment of another changes the situation."

—CAROLINE MYSS, *THE ENERGETICS OF HEALING* (AUDIOBOOK)

Take Your Gifts Along on Your Journey

You are a soul, housed in a physical body having a spiritual experience. You are here to love and cherish your gifts. The experiences in your life have all been opportunities for you to clear, complete, and work through what holds you back from vibrating love. Anxiety and its symptoms restrained your energy and in doing so may have fueled an addiction to fear. Notice what emotions appear in front of you and the internal response to what you see. If you are fearful or worried, or believe you have somehow failed, celebrate this insight by respecting and then purifying your energy.

This final chapter is about cutting ties with energy that interferes with your ability to support others without losing yourself. When you tighten or brace yourself for what appears to be a tremendous obstacle or arduous journey, your gifts feel temporary. Respecting your soul's journey is about the embodiment of unconditional love. There is no magic pill that will ever take all pain away. But your soul is not afraid of pain. Your soul knows that pain is an emotion that you can face and purify like any other. Your soul wants to relinquish the need to survive your experiences and relationships through fear alone. It wants you to learn about love. The individuals and circumstances that float your way are all part of a larger plan to support your growth to embodying love. As this occurs, sharing your gifts is not something you actively do, but rather an energy that flows from you all the time. Therefore, your focus will shift from wanting to help others feel better to valuing your moments of flow.

Before delving into your soul's journey it is important for you to know that your gifts are made of the same material the universe is made of: energy, vibration, and matter. You already have these gifts inside you. Therefore, it is not your job to give other people their gifts, nor is it your duty to help them search for them. This approach will only occupy your mind, thus dimming your vibration. Each and every soul is here to learn, grow, and contribute energy to the planet. Opportunities via events and experiences are provided along the way, some more arduous than others. Nonetheless, one of the most common experiences human beings share is loss. Loss takes on many forms, including loss of life, dignity, love, pride, and at times, hope. It is natural to want to stop and control this force of loss—whether for yourself or another person—as it can be not only painful but frightening.

The soul is an infinite source of love and light. When you disconnect from this part of yourself—through anxiety or any other issue—that loss becomes a constant companion to your nervous system and cells. While reading this chapter, reflect on the moments where supporting others felt difficult or emotionally draining. If you hear yourself repeat in your head or out loud, *I try*, pause and notice the energy behind those words. *I try to be a good husband. I try to be a good parent. I try to be a good daughter. I try* is often pulsated by fear and doubt. The journey of your soul is not separate from others'. This means how you interact with the present moment influences how much or little you are consciously or unconsciously sharing your gifts.

To share your gifts means to share your vibration, and it is through your energy that you can be a tremendous support to others. For example, it is not uncommon for people going through a challenging time to post on Facebook or send out an email asking for the prayers of others. Are they asking you to pray in fear? No, what they are asking is to pray not only for divine intervention but also for your higher vibrations to be directed their way. The collection of strong vibrational energy supported by loving intentions has the potential to create powerful interventions.

Now, this certainly does not mean you should wait until someone posts something on Facebook before sending love her way. Sharing your gifts is unconditional. It is not something you necessarily do, but rather a way to live your life. Since you are human, you can pick up on the energy of others easily. If you sense someone is angry, depressed, or hurting you have the ability to send her love or compassionate energy at any time. The key is that these vibrations will come across strong if you send them while you are experiencing them yourself. For example, I have a daily meditation practice. Due to a busy household, this practice varies in length. However, by applying the practices in Chapters 4–6, I have learned how to quickly lift and spread out my vibrations. As I feel the sensations circulate in my body, I imagine loving images such as beautiful places I like to visit. Sometimes I just imagine the word *love*. I direct this energy to my family and I also send it to all the new babies in the hospital, to their families, and to hospital staff. I personally had a very difficult first birth. I was unable to walk due to the fact that I couldn't feel my legs for forty-eight hours. (The doctors panicked and within hours after giving birth to my first daughter I was getting MRI scans to see if and what nerves were damaged. To this day, occasionally one of my legs gives out while I'm walking.) When a family is in the midst of a significant life transition, experiences like these can start them out on shaky ground. Therefore, when I send these intentions, they come from my gift of empathy as well as my gratitude that everything worked out fine.

As you become competent in these types of practices, it is natural for you to want to share them. Not only will you be a carrier of the gifts, but also a teacher. It will be important for you to watch how you share the information. If you share information when you are feeling irritable or frustrated, or because you feel it is your duty to guide others, it may not be as well received. It is far more impactful when you share from the vibration of love rather than just the thought alone. Therefore, it is important that you take time each day to strengthen these higher vibrations (love, joy, appreciation) in you so that when you do state these words, you feel them. As you feel them, you inevitably transfer them out into the world. You will not only impact others by what you say but also who you are. Once these vibrations are elicited, here are some ways to share:

- Sharing can be as simple as saying, *This is such a beautiful day* or *Thank you for helping me.* When you share your gratitude, you are sharing your gifts.
- You may also share through modeling. For example, you could say something out loud like, *I just felt myself getting anxious, but I took some long, deep breaths for about the time it takes me to brush my teeth and I was able to diminish it. Normally I would have reacted or said something negative, but I found that breathing really helped.*
- You can also share through prayer circles or similar events. When my father decided to undergo spine surgery, my children were still in school and I elected not to drive the four hours to be with him. Since I could not be with him the night before his surgery, I attended a prayer circle. I entered his name into the circle and six other people and I prayed for him.

As you can see, you can share directly or indirectly. In other words, the person does not need to know you are helping him. Sharing your gifts is a win-win situation. By pausing and eliciting vibrations of compassion and gratitude before sending it forward, both you, as the sender, and the receiver benefit. In my opinion, there is nothing greater than that.

Respecting the Soul's Journey

Every soul is meant to move along through its journey in its own way, in its own time frame and unique circumstances. How your journey unfolds can impact others'. Yet you can never be in charge of someone else's evolution. If you consciously or unconsciously believe that you are fully in charge of the course of others, recognize and clear this belief. This belief:

- Supports unrealistic expectations
- Places a tremendous responsibility on your shoulders
- May prevent you from both asking and receiving help from the divine

When you do ask for help, your efforts may appear unanswered. In this case, consider asking yourself if your requests are unrealistic and if in some way they disrespect the journey of others.

Establish Your Expectations

The first step of respecting the soul's journey is to take into account what you are willing to accept, as far as the temperament, personality traits, viewpoints, or choices of another. Also, what behaviors are you willing or not willing to allow? This means part of the process of sharing your gifts is knowing when to set boundaries. Think of your energy as a precious commodity. As a practitioner of energy, I have experienced this firsthand. For example, I might offer my service at a discount or even for free. If, for example, a person shows up late or cancels at the last minute, I know immediately that she may not fully understand the value of energy. I will then set a boundary. Perhaps I won't call her and just accept that she has let the opportunity pass. Other times, I may call and let her know I need to charge more for the service to make up for the cancellation—it all depends on the situation.

Other times, boundaries need to be set when someone takes up a great deal of your time. Perhaps someone confides in you a great deal. Notice how you feel when you leave this person. If you feel drained or irritated, consider that you might have unconsciously shared or drained too much energy. Other examples include overbooking yourself, saying yes when you really want to say no, and believing that it is not acceptable to change your mind. Pay attention to how you might create stories to save face. When you are not truthful, you are likely to lose energy. If you find yourself lying frequently to someone in your life, you may need to take a look at that relationship and whether it belongs in your life. No one really needs to know why you have chosen to cancel your dinner plans—a simple response of *Something came up* or *I can't make it this time, sorry* is enough. If you are tired or your soul is craving an evening of quiet, trust me, you will be a much better gift sharer if you listen to your own body.

If there are certain things that you are not willing to allow, are you really focusing on the other person's journey or yours? For example, if you are not a fan of gossip yet find yourself maintaining a relationship with someone who thrives off it, you are engaging in behaviors that are counterproductive to your purpose and your truth. At some point you have to ask yourself, *Am I really sharing my gifts with this person or is this relationship feeding a counterproductive belief in me?* Perhaps you believe if you let go of this relationship, you will regret it later, or that ending it would be mean or hurtful to the other person. If the situation is eliciting certain emotions in you, then this is not about sharing your gifts; it is about something in you that needs attention. When you choose not to set boundaries, such as limiting your exposure to this person, it not only interferes with the growth of others but also inhibits your ability to manifest the things you most desire as well as the conscious connection to your gifts. Rather than focusing your energy on that particular person, consider sharing your gifts in other ways. Acts of kindness, gratitude, or volunteer work are some of the most respectful ways to support another soul.

When Jerry went to do errands with his daughter, he felt grumpy and annoyed. He thought of all the other things he could and would prefer to do with his Saturday. Although he drove his teenage daughter to school every morning, while shopping he suddenly found himself relaxing and enjoying the experience. The act of shopping was not what he was enjoying, but rather it was the experience of being around his daughter who, at that time, felt energetically relaxed and open. He hadn't experienced that side of her often due to the pressure of homework and the daily rush of getting to school. This experience stayed with him to the point where he even spoke about it with his wife. By relaxing and being present in the moment, Jerry was in fact sharing his gifts.

Every Moment Is Significant

You would assume that the soul's journey is mostly impacted by momentous events, such as getting married, graduating, or beginning a new career. Yet in reality, some of the most significant moments that shape and in some cases reset the direction of your soul are so subtle that you could easily miss them. Respecting your soul's journey means to trust that you are being guided in your own special way. Every moment is significant—even the ones that don't necessarily feel good.

Respecting your soul's journey means you will spend less time worrying or attending to how and in what way others are developing and more attention to your own spiritual development. Focusing on yourself helps you relinquish emotions that stem from judgment and the need to control.

Gift Tag

Meditation: Tree Gazing

Lying on your back under a tree looking up at the sky in a park or your backyard can be very meditative. Notice how your body feels as it lies upon the earth. With your legs extended, gaze up at the tree branches as you inhale and exhale deeply through your nose. Soften your eyes and notice the colors of the leaves and branches. Notice the sky and clouds surrounding it. Feel the temperature of the ground on your skin. Just relax and see yourself and the tree as one—almost like the tree is a friend you are choosing to sit and spend time with. Smile at the tree and notice how it smiles back. As you keep breathing and observing, notice how you are sharing your gifts with this tree.

Now, roll to one side and stand up. Stand directly under this same tree. Look down at your feet and notice how they are positioned. Notice if one foot is pointing out more than the other. Straighten your feet out side by side so they are parallel. Imagine them like headlights. If they are pointed too far to the left or right, the "car" may crash. Through sensing and feeling make your feet straight. As you move them in this direction, see yourself shining the headlights on the course of your own soul. Notice if your feet fall out of place or revert to old habits. Once again, while breathing in through your nose and exhaling out through your nose, intentionally place your feet on course. As you do this, pay attention to the sensations on your feet. As you draw your attention to the soles of your feet, you may notice a tingly sensation. This sensation is the same vibration that sets you on course. Even more so than your thoughts and the happenings around you, it is your vibration that is the director of your soul. Take a minute and allow yourself to become familiar with this vibration. As you meditate on your own, you are likely to become soothed through your personal vibration rather than through the temporary adrenaline you may receive from running the road of others. As you walk away from the tree, continue your meditation. You now take it with you, one step at a time as you walk forward while grounding your vibrations in the present moment.

Allow Others' Gifts to Reveal Themselves

Self-esteem is something you can build over time through skill development and accomplishments and through your acceptance of it. It cannot, however, be given to you by another person. You can influence the self-esteem of others by raising your vibration so that the emotions of acceptance and appreciation become part of your experience. If you were giving someone constructive feedback, most schools of thought would encourage you to notice the good first before mentioning the areas for growth. Self-esteem works in a similar way. You notice the good; however, some of the best teachers are able to see space for growth. There is always more to learn and develop in the human experience. When it comes to sharing your gifts, think of the old saying "The customer is always right." For example, if a patron's food does not taste good at a restaurant, the manager is better off giving the customer the benefit of the doubt rather than arguing with him. The same is true for the gifts. You cannot give someone her gifts—just like you cannot convince someone what medium-rare looks like—but you can teach about the gifts through your example of how you handle the circumstances that come your way.

As you practice the techniques taught in Chapters 4–6 as well as the Gift Tags throughout this book, you will come to appreciate the power of the human body. Your breath when noticed, encouraged, and allowed to expand and contract has the capacity to move you into a state where you can truly feel your emotions and embrace love. Just as anxiety is contagious, so is consciousness. When you are aware of your breathing, vibrations, and energy, you spread that awareness into the world around you.

When Mark and Mary fought, they had a habit of bringing up the past and blaming each other for what was not going right in their relationship. Each felt the other wasn't doing enough to make the changes the marriage needed to become healthier. When Mark was upset, Mary tried her best to keep her mouth shut. In the midst of it, she would tell herself to keep quiet and ignore what he was saying. She would also silently hear herself say what a jerk she thought he was being and how immature he was. Her choice to remain silent prevented things from escalating but did not seem to change anything beyond that.

Once Mary learned to tune in to her own vibration, things started to change. Each morning, she would begin her day by breathing and intentionally choosing the thoughts she wanted to put into her day. The next time she started to bicker with Mark she handled it differently. Rather than trying to ignore him and push him away with her own thoughts, she allowed herself to dive into her own vibration. She did this by closing her eyes and exhaling by pressing her navel toward her spine. She kept exhaling as if she were anchoring her spirit into her physical body. Normally, when bickering took place, she would easily drift off and abandon her body. This time, she chose to stay in her physical body and connect to the vibration of her soul.

When it comes to experiencing your emotions, the effects are subtle. To go directly from anger to peace, particularly in the beginning, is not realistic. Instead, imagine Mark went from worrying, to anger, to demanding, and finally to becoming more neutral. When you are both engaging and sharing your gifts, always know progress is being made—it just may not be in the way you expect it. One day, Mary's husband texted her to let her know he had made an appointment to see a therapist. This was a tremendous shift for Mark, as he had been adamantly against it in the past. Mark had clearly received her calming energy, which gave him the courage to seek out help.

Had Mary responded to Mark in the old way, she would have put out a vibration of fear and control. Instead, Mary had been planting the seeds of her vibrational requests into her daily practice. When couples focus on who is right and who is wrong, this immobilizes the gift energy. Connecting to your vibration lightens the moment. Even though the situation may appear identical in behavior, the vibration has altered. As you learn to trust this occurrence, you will be able to notice and observe the vibrational changes. If you expect an immediate or pronounced shift in your life, you are too attached to the outcome. Trust in the universe and its powers.

Gift Tag

Exercise: Create Your Day

Before running out the door in the morning, take a moment to sit down, close your eyes, and create your ideal day. As you inhale and exhale, imagine all the things you would like to put into your day. Keep in mind words are vibrations. See yourself writing the words on a chalkboard, or having them flash in your mind's eye as you state them. For example, *I choose to create love, laughter, patience, creativity, and wisdom.* You may also state, *I choose to connect to my gifts.*

How to Support Others

Supporting others on their journey to find their gifts is humbling, fulfilling, and a privilege. By choosing to focus and develop your own energy, you become a vibrational assistant to others. To do this well it is important to watch yourself:

- Notice how you interpret what you see around you.
- Avoid making comparisons or assuming individuals on other paths need healing or redirection. People are creators of their own vibration.

Everyone has the ability to create, but not everyone has been shown the tools for supporting their vibration throughout the peaks and valleys life brings. This section discusses three ways to support others: playing in the gift vibration, promoting a sense of belonging, and delivery.

Playing with Your Gifts

One of the best ways to support others is to encourage opportunities to play in the gift vibration. Yes, playing! Picture it like playing in the rain. Ask the person who you are supporting what she loves to do and when she feels most connected and alive. It may be movement, stillness, creativity, nature, animals, mechanics, travel, music, etc. Then offer to do that activity with her. If someone is in an environment where she is not permitted or provided enough opportunity to feel joy, she may mistakenly take on the emotions of others. Feelings of unworthiness, discontent, and anxiety may be absorbed, sapping any motivation to try anything that will lift her emotions.

Individuals in a vibrationally draining environment will benefit from developing small, yet consistent practices that lighten their energy. Here are some examples:

- Employers may consider encouraging employees to take a break outside by setting up benches and tables.

- Parents may encourage their child to take one extracurricular activity rather than three to keep space in the schedule for downtime and creativity.
- Partners may develop a practice of taking three deep breaths before entering the door after work.
- Schools may choose to focus on building strengths rather than preventing weaknesses.

Once space is created, let the playfulness emerge. Think of your energy as a low-lit flame. As you expand your belly on inhale and contract it on exhale, allow yourself to be lighthearted. Move your body in spontaneous ways. Children do this naturally, as they might be standing one minute and then suddenly do a twirl or kick. In that moment, they are playing with their gifts.

Making time to laugh and celebrate the day are other ways to interact in this vibration. Think of yourself as a vibrational assistant. Notice when someone could use some company, a walk, or simply a hand. Just by holding the door open for someone, letting another car go ahead of you, or smiling at a stranger, you become an attendant to the gifts. Keep in mind, you are not giving them their esteem or their gifts—they already have them. You are simply providing them with a lift so they can sense their own direction.

Promote a Sense of Belonging

Abraham Maslow was one of the first psychologists to identify the road to self-actualization, which he defined as reaching one's fullest potential. Inherent in this concept is the need for all human beings to feel a sense of belonging before moving toward self-actualization. As consciousness evolves, human beings learn how to tune in to their energy more than their thoughts as a means for developing this. This shift also impacts how you support others.

When people feel as if they don't belong, it is an indication that they are functioning off low energy. In many cases, their energetic flow is being blocked by unconscious memories of feeling uncomfortable in their own bodies. As a result, people-pleasing and people-proving behaviors may surface. For example, a parent buys her child things in an attempt to keep him happy. Another example would be a person who attempts to prove her worth by attempting to change how others see her. Perhaps she works harder—to the point of burning herself out—trying to reach the expectations of others (even if they are unreachable).

To support others, it is important that you be mindful of your reactions. Watch yourself for quick or panicky responses. Signing your child up for another activity to promote a sense of belonging may be a good idea—however, notice if it is a response that stems from low energy. As you support others it is a good rule of thumb to increase your vibration (see Chapter 4) before making a decision or taking action. That way, you know your decision is coming from a place of purpose and truth, not fear or judgment. The following table shows the difference between offering help by doing something for someone and allowing your energy to lead the way.

Doing	Sharing
Giving advice on what someone should do	Relaxing your body, and sending positive intentions
Based on your discomfort	Based on your love
Feeling like you are pressed to help	Trusting that your vibrations and intentions are enough

Energetic belonging is when you feel connected to your heart and spirit. It is when your energy is soft and playful. Imagine yourself as a child jumping rope. See yourself swinging the rope around you as you hop up and down. In that moment, a child does not question whether she belongs—she just jumps. A sense of belonging is based on how well energy is invested in that moment. The more energy you have in your body, the more you belong. The following example illustrates this further.

Although Leeann had many friends, a family, and a career, inwardly she struggled with feeling a sense of belonging. She felt out of place and at times uncomfortable in her own skin. This left her feeling sad and discontent. Once Leeann was able to learn how a sense of belonging is developed energetically within the body, she was able to let go of trying to fit in. Before doing this, however, she needed to give herself permission to release all the times she felt out of place. While closing her eyes and sitting in a relaxed position, she gave herself permission to reflect on this topic. What she realized was she had felt out of place most of her life, including in her family, at church, among friends, in school, and even at work.

Leeann set the intention to clear all the times she felt she did not belong. Because she liked yoga, she turned to it to help her clear her emotions. Lying on her back, she put her feet on the floor (with her knees bent, hip-width apart) and lifted her bum off the floor into a yoga pose called bridge. As she pressed into the heels of her feet this stimulated her in breath (belly rising to the ceiling) as well as her out breath (navel moving toward her spine). She held this pose for five breaths and as she allowed her spine to relax on the floor while stretching out her feet, she felt soothed by her own bodily sensation. In the moment, she created a new association of belonging as a state of energetic abundance.

When people feel out of place, it is not uncommon for them to drop half of their energy around them. Most likely it is the energy that is typically housed in the lower half of the body (below your navel). In the previous example, Leeann was able to clear the energy that held her back while reinstalling new associations to belonging by intentionally positioning herself in bridge pose. Leeann was able to see how many of her relationships were reflections of not feeling like she belonged. Acknowledging and clearing this allowed her to spend less time blaming others and her situation, and more time tuning in to developing her gifts. This gave her mind something new to focus on, allowing her to stimulate vibrations that cultivated her sense of gratitude for how she belonged in her body and on this planet. This is a way to support yourself. The following Gift Tag is a way you can indirectly help others.

Gift Tag

Skill: Seeing Breathing

If you have ever been around someone who is stuck in his anger or frustration, you know how separate you may feel from this person. No matter what you say or do, you are unable to make a connection. Quit trying, and instead take some deep breaths, expanding your belly on inhale and contracting it on exhale. Now visualize the person you would like to support. This may be a friend, family member, or even a stranger. Visualize him in your mind and imagine his belly, like yours, taking deep exaggerated breaths. Picture the organs inside his midsection. Visualize his lungs and kidneys expanding and contracting inside a beautiful white light. Watch his belly rise up and down. Do this for up to sixty seconds and pretend just for a moment that he too is breathing in this way, as if it were truly happening. See this person making healthy choices.

Deliver Your Energy

How you choose to share your gifts makes a difference. Focus on the energy behind your actions rather than what you will say or do. If you come from a fearful, worried, or controlling vibration, people will sense this and become afraid or defensive. As a result, an energetic exchange of fear begins to occur. To break the cycle, it is important to focus on your own vibration before moving forward.

Low-Energy Response	Gift Delivery
Driven to respond quickly	Sense the energy first before responding
Thought-driven	Receive reassurance through feeling
Talking too much or repeating oneself	Pausing or doing a self-check between words
Blaming	Noticing

Responses such as talking too much, repeating yourself, yelling, and blaming can spoil your efforts. As a result, you may not only feel worse but also separate from your true intentions. Taking time to center yourself daily can prevent you from inadvertently setting someone off course. As always, less is more. This means you do not always have to say something when you're supporting someone. It is more important for you to pay attention to yourself than it is to try to "solve" problems. Listening closely to a person and saying something like, "This sounds like a tough time for you. I'm here to support you. What can I do to help?" shows the person that you're not going to solve her problems, but you are "on her side." To do this, give yourself time to digest a thought fully by allowing it to transform into a feeling. This creates space between one thought and another. The key is knowing that thoughts can only be fully digested in the body, not the mind.

Lauren was a mother of a six-year-old girl. One day, her daughter came running into the house in tears. When Lauren asked her what was wrong she replied, "I can't do things as well as my sisters." The mother then got down on her knees and looked her daughter in the eyes. She asked her daughter where she felt it in her body. Her six-year-old pointed to her belly. Lauren hugged her, and as she did this, rather than thinking *Poor baby* and frowning, she instead smiled. By smiling instead of frowning, it was impossible for Lauren to think thoughts such as *Poor baby*. Instead, she found she didn't think much at all. She focused on how good her daughter felt in her arms. In other words, in that moment Lauren was choosing to support her daughter through her own higher vibrations. She recognized the power of her own smile muscles and how the body automatically interprets this expression (by sending out calming chemicals) as love.

In this example, Lauren could have easily embraced her daughter because she felt bad and wanted to make her feel better. But deep down, people don't want to be cured, rescued, or fixed; they want to be loved. By approaching from love rather than rescuing, you mirror one of the highest vibrations of the human experience. This is more powerful than anything you could ever say or do.

Choose Love

If you think of anxiety as something you wish to beat, control, or get rid of, you're pulling a heaviness into your heart. The more you instead play in the gift energy you have inside you, the less likely you are to revert to old responses that contribute to a cycle of suppressing emotions.

Instead, hold your energy dear by choosing to focus on what is in the present moment. What you were and what you hope to be are no longer relevant. Even if the situation, emotion, or experience is coated with vibrations of fear, embrace each as it is and trust that your gifts will follow in due time. This mindset elevates your vibration, opening up opportunity for you to both release and reinstall new states of mind. You are an energetic being and you have the opportunity and privilege of experiencing how these gifts are represented in your life.

Take time to reflect on how purpose, empathy, resiliency, and hope may surface today in your life. Plant the intention to water your gifts regularly. Fertilize each with your beliefs, breath, and faith. Watch for the expressions of your gifts in your life—notice the various packages they arrive in. When you feel challenged or defeated by your perceived mishaps, take a moment to ask yourself what you are devoted to: anxiety or the maturation of your gifts.

My hope is that after reading this book, you are never able to look at the symptoms of anxiety in the same way—that you are able to seek out and call forth your energy fearlessly. May your knowledge and interest in the gifts take precedence and may you fully embrace the opportunity to choose differently.

Gift Tag

Meditation: You Are a Light

Take a moment, close your eyes, and imagine a beam of light or a rising star. See yourself as you are today, placing the lower vibrations of guilt, shame, unworthiness, panic, fear, and despair into the palm of your hand and raising them up to a light. The light represents peace, joy, and enlightenment. Now, while still visualizing yourself, take a moment and give thanks for all the experiences and emotions that have led you to this point. Offer them your gratitude and blessings, and release the energy (now in the form of a star) into the universe. Watch the star rise up beyond where you can see it—beyond the clouds, way out into the atmosphere. Take a moment and consider that a piece of you that you no longer choose to hang on to is now released and that it has transformed into light and now shines upon you and the earth.

As you complete this chapter, take a moment and thank the universe for the emotions that innocently protected you. Give thanks for the opportunity to view and choose differently. May you choose love and may this final Gift Tag bring forth for you and those around you peace from the symptoms of anxiety.

With love and sincerity, your gift assistant,

Sherianna

REFERENCES

Ablow, Keith. *Living the Truth: Transform Your Life Through the Power of Insight and Honesty.* New York: Hachette Book Group, 2007.

A.D.A.M. "Stress and Anxiety." *New York Times,* March 27, 2014. *www.nytimes.com/health/guides/symptoms/stress-and-anxiety/possible-complications.html.*

A Course in Miracles. "About." *https://acim.org/AboutACIM/.*

Anxiety and Depression Association of America. "Understanding the Facts of Anxiety Disorders and Depression Is the First Step." *www.adaa.org/understanding-anxiety.*

Anxiety and Depression Association of America. "Stress." *www.adaa.org/understanding-anxiety/related-illnesses/stress.*

Attuned Vibrations. "528 Hz: The Love Frequency." *http://attunedvibrations.com/528hz/.*

The Chopra Center. "What Is a Mantra?" *www.chopra.com/ccl meditation/21dmc/mantra.html.*

The Chopra Center. "The Law of Least Effort." *www.chopra.com/community/online-library/the-seven-spiritual-laws-of-success/the-law-of-least-effort.*

Chopra, Deepak. "The Law of Least Effort." Spirit Library. July 5, 2008. *http://spiritlibrary.com/deepak-chopra/the-law-of-least-effort.*

Chopra, Deepak. *The Seven Spiritual Laws of Success: A Practical Guide to the Fulfillment of Your Dreams.* San Rafael, CA: Amber-Allen Publishing, 1994.

Dale, Cyndi. "The Outer Chakras: The Energy Centers that Connect You to the Universe." Sounds True. *www .soundstrue.com/shop/articles/The_Outer_Chakras-The_Energy_Centers_that_Connect_You_to_the_Universe_with_Cyndi_Dale?component=authorcontent.*

Dispenza, Joe. *Breaking the Habit of Being Yourself: How to Lose Your Mind and Create a New One.* Carlsbad, CA: Hay House, Inc., 2013.

Dyer, Wayne W. *Getting in the Gap: Making Conscious Contact with God Through Meditation.* Carlsbad, CA: Hay House, Inc., 2003.

Dyer, Wayne W. *The Power of Intention.* Carlsbad, CA: Hay House, Inc., 2004.

Earnest, Michelle. "Energy Medicine Techniques to Relieve Stress and Anxiety." Handout, Fredericksburg Complementary Therapies. *http://fredericksburgcomplementarytherapies.com/yahoo_site_admin/assets/docs/stress_and_anxiety_handout.360053.pdf.*

Eden, Donna, and David Feinstein, PhD. *Energy Medicine.* New York, NY: Penguin Group, 2008.

Edwards, Bridget. "Namaste and Sawubona, a Zulu greeting." *http://bridgie8.hubpages.com/hub/Namaste-and-Sawubona-a-Zulu-greeting.*

Emoto, Masaru. *The Hidden Messages in Water.* Hillsboro, OR: Beyond Words Publishing, Inc., 2004.

Godwin, Joscelyn, ed. *Cosmic Music: Musical Keys to the Interpretation of Reality.* Rochester, VT: Inner Traditions International, 1989. *www.biowaves.com/Info/WhatIsSound.php.*

Hawkins, David R. *Along the Path to Enlightenment.* Edited by Scott Jeffrey. Carlsbad, CA: Hay House, Inc., 2011.

Hawkins, David R. *Power vs. Force: The Hidden Determinants of Human Behavior.* Carlsbad, CA: Hay House, Inc., 2012.

Hay, Louise L. *You Can Heal Your Life.* Carlsbad, CA: Hay House, Inc., 2004.

Horwitz, Allan V. *Anxiety: A Short History.* Baltimore: Johns Hopkins University Press, 2013.

Iyengar, B.K.S. *Light on Life: The Yoga Journey to Wholeness, Inner Peace, and Ultimate Freedom.* New York: Rodale Books, 2005.

Kabat-Zinn, Jon. "The Mindfulness Revolution." TIME, February 3, 2014. *http://content.time.com/time/magazine/article/0,9171,2163560,00.html.*

Life, David. "To Infinity and Beyond!" Yoga Journal, May–June 2000. *www.yogajournal.com/practice/217.*

Maraboli, Steve. *Unapologetically You: Reflections on Life and the Human Experience.* Port Washington, NY: A Better Today Publishing, 2013.

Marae, Zoe. Lecture presented at the Embodied Love Series, Cape Cod, MA, 2011.

McLean, Sarah. *Soul Centered: Transform Your Life in 8 Weeks with Meditation.* Carlsbad, CA: Hay House, Inc., 2012.

Moorjani, Anita. *Dying to Be Me: My Journey from Cancer, to Near Death, to True Healing.* Carlsbad, CA: Hay House, Inc., 2012.

Myss, Caroline. "Difference Between Ego and Soul Service." *IET Evolve* (video blog). January 9, 2010. *www.ietevolve.com/2010/01/difference-between-ego-and-soul-service.html.*

Myss, Caroline. *The Energetics of Healing*. Louisville, CO. Sounds True, 2004. DVD.

Nelson, Bradley. *The Emotion Code*. Mesquite, NV: Wellness Unmasked Publishing, 2007.

Newberg, Andrew, and Mark Robert Waldman. *Words Can Change Your Brain*. New York: Hudson Street Press, 2012.

NurrieStearns, Mary, and Rick NurrieStearns. *Yoga for Anxiety: Meditations and Practices for Calming the Body and Mind*. Oakland, CA: New Harbinger Publications, 2010.

Ortner, Nick. *The Tapping Solution: A Revolutionary System for Stress-Free Living*. Carlsbad, CA: Hay House, Inc., 2013.

Powers, Sarah. *Insight Yoga*. Boston: Shambhala Publications, 2008.

Powers, Sarah. Insight Yoga Workshop, Church of Holy Christ, Orleans, MA, July 27–28, 2012.

Riess, Helen. "The Power of Empathy." Lecture presented at TEDx Middlebury, December 19, 2013. Video available at *http://tedxtalks.ted.com/video/The-power-of-empathy-Helen-Ries; search%3Atag%3A"TEDxMiddlebury*.

Sparrow, Patti. *Stepping Stones*. Photography by Kathleen Warren. Franklin, MA: Nature Woman Wisdom Press, 2012.

Taylor, Jill Bolte. *My Stroke of Insight: A Brain Scientist's Personal Journey*. New York: Penguin Group, 2006.

Vitelli, Romeo. "Learning to Be Resilient." *Psychology Today*, May 13, 2013. *www.psychologytoday.com/blog/media-spotlight/201305/ learning-be-resilient*.

Warren, Rick. *The Purpose Driven Life: What on Earth Am I Here For?* Grand Rapids: Zondervan, 2002.

Williamson, Marianne. *A Return to Love.* New York: Harper Collins Publishers, 1992.

Williams, Mark, John Teasdale, Zindel Segal, and Jon Kabat-Zinn. *The Mindful Way Through Depression: Freeing Yourself from Chronic Unhappiness.* New York: Guildford Press, 2007.

Zukav, Gary, and Linda Francis. *The Heart of the Soul: Emotional Awareness.* New York: Free Press, 2001.

INDEX